THE TOP ONE HUNDRED ITALIAN DISHES

THE TOP ONE HUNDRED ITALIAN DISHES
DIANE SEED

EBURY PRESS

London

For Antonio Mary

I wish it's gonna "start"
for you the best part of
your life (Just now!)
good good Luck &
(stay)" in the wolf's mouth
— italian proverb.

Jens

First published in Great Britain in 1991
by Ebury Press
an imprint of the
Random Century Group Limited
Random Century House
20 Vauxhall Bridge Road
London SW1V 2SA

Text copyright © Diane Seed 1991
Illustrations © Simon & Schuster Australia

The right of Diane Seed to be identified as the author of this
work has been asserted by her in accordance with the Copyright,
Designs and Patents Act 1988.

Designed and illustrated by Helen Semmler

British Library Cataloguing-in-Publication Data

Seed, Diane
  The top 100 Italian dishes.
  I. Title
  641.5945

ISBN 0-09-175033-4

Typeset in Australia by Asset Typesetting Pty Ltd
Produced by Mandarin Offset in Hong Kong

CONTENTS

INTRODUCTION

ITALIANS LOVE TO EAT, and they have an innate sense of hospitality. Their spontaneous warmth is one of the factors that contributes to the success of Italian restaurants all over the world. Food is prepared with care and affection. Good quality fresh, seasonal produce is regarded as essential and the natural flavour of food is never masked with complicated sauces. The culinary tradition of Italy is based on vegetables, cereals, fish and olive oil: a healthy way of eating which appeals to modern tastes.

Today Italy enjoys comparative prosperity, but in the past large areas suffered under centuries of foreign rule, and hunger was an ever-present enemy. The people learned to make the most of whatever ingredients were available and wild or homegrown vegetables, and bread often provided a complete meal. The traditional cooking of the poor, known as the *cucina povera,* used care and imagination to make simple ingredients festive. Expensive items like eggs and cheese were used sparingly, and vegetables, herbs and olive oil played the dominant role. In the southern region around Puglia, for example, round or square *friselle* were made from whole wheat flour or oats, and baked hard so that they would keep indefinitely. It was not unusual for the evening meal to be *friselle* dipped in water to soften them slightly, then heaped with chopped ripe tomatoes and good olive oil.

Pasta has become an international favourite, so much so that most households would have a packet of pasta lurking in the kitchen. Non-Italians tend to make a complete meal of pasta and salad. However in Italy today pasta is eaten as a first course, followed by meat or fish and a vegetable dish.

Often an appetiser or *antipasto* is served before the pasta and the meal is completed by fresh fruit or a dessert, *dolce.* Some people even enjoy a plate of cheese before the dessert. Visitors to Italy are often amazed by the quantity of food consumed in one meal and can usually get no further than the pasta course.

For years I was convinced that pasta was the only course worth eating in Italian restaurants because the meat and fish dishes seemed so predictable. It was after I discovered regional home-cooking that I became truly enthusiastic about other courses and could lament the dearth of interesting main courses on restaurant menus. In the last few years, however, many chefs have painstakingly researched forgotten regional recipes, adapting them to suit modern tastes, so that today's menus offer a greater variety and pasta now has some strong competition.

This collection of recipes represents some of my personal favourites most of which are not easy to find outside Italy. The book is divided into sections according to the main ingredient. The quantities given in the recipes are for six people if the dish is served in its usual place on the Italian menu. If you are serving pasta or rice as a one-dish meal, you may like to increase the quantities. Indeed, all the recipes are versatile: each dish can be cooked as a one-course meal, appetiser or main course, according to your personal preference. I have not included desserts because fresh fruit makes the perfect ending to most Italian meals.

The Italians have survived their troubled past by perfecting the art of *arrangiarsi* — adapting themselves to the prevailing circumstances. If you cannot find a certain ingredient, improvise and use what is available. The dish will taste different, but it will have your personal touch and this too is part of the Italian tradition.

Happy cooking and *Buon Appetito.*

PASTA, RICE AND PIZZA

PASTA, RICE AND PIZZA

ITALY HAS ONLY existed as a unified country for 130 years, so traditional Italian cooking tends to be regional rather than national. The first Italian restaurants were opened abroad in the last century when poverty caused a mass emigration from the south of Italy. The immigrants took their culture with them, introducing the world to their regional dishes like pizza and spaghetti.

Since Roman times, southern Italy has been regarded as the country's granary. Naples became the centre for commercially produced pasta since good durum wheat was grown in that area and the hot winds from Vesuvius combined with the cool sea breezes to provide the right climate for drying the sheets of dough. The Italians were quick to adopt this cheap and versatile ingredient after its invention, flavouring it with olive oil and any vegetables or seafood available.

The area in the middle of Italy around Emilia has always enjoyed comparative prosperity and there is a note of opulence in the cooking of that region. This is the home of the rich egg pasta which was invented on the occasion of Lucrezia Borgia's marriage to the Duke of Ferrara. The court chef, Zafirano, made thin sheets of yellow pasta and cut them into curls as a compliment to her golden ringlets. This pasta is the most suited to delicate cream and butter-based sauces.

Pizza is an even more ancient Italian tradition than pasta, and it too originated in southern Italy. The original pizzas were tasty breads baked in wood-fired stone ovens. Olives, tomatoes or onions were added to enrich the dough until, eventually each area of the country had its own speciality. Pizza developed naturally from this type of bread and became an economical one-course meal.

The good rice grown in the fertile Po Valley has inspired a tradition of rice cooking in the areas around Milan and Venice where rice is used, instead of pasta, to make nourishing broths and where risottos are enriched with local vegetables and seafood. Rice was not grown in the south of Italy and the only southern recipes using rice were introduced by the ruling Spaniards.

LINGUINE WITH PRAWNS (SHRIMP) AND ROCKET

Linguine gamberi e rughetta

Tomato sauce (see Aubergine
    (Eggplant) Timbales with
    Tomato and Basil Sauce, page
    49, but omit the basil leaves)
Cayenne pepper
50 g (1¾ oz) rocket
30 mL (2 tablespoons) olive oil
1 kg (2 lb) prawns (shrimp),
    shelled and deveined, heads
    reserved
Parsley, chopped
Salt
2 red tomatoes, peeled and cubed
500 g (1 lb) linguine

THIS RECIPE COMES from the beautiful Positano hotel, Le Sirenuse, owned by the Sersale family who organise regular pasta festivals where their chefs prepare old family recipes and enchanting innovations.

Method: Make the basic tomato sauce adding a good pinch of cayenne pepper.

If you are using cultivated rocket leave a handful to be added just before serving. Chop the rest roughly and add when the sauce is cooked. If you are using the bitter, spiky wild rocket remove the stalks but leave the leaves whole. These should be cooked in the tomato sauce for 5 minutes. You can also add the washed prawn heads to add flavour to the sauce. These can be removed before serving or left in according to your personal preference.

In a large pan or wok heat the oil and cook the prawns, adding the parsley, salt and a pinch of cayenne pepper. Cook for 5 minutes then add the tomato sauce and the cubed tomato.

Cook the pasta in boiling salted water until it is not quite tender. Drain and stir into the sauce. Allow the pasta to absorb the flavour of the sauce in these last few minutes of cooking, then add the handful of cultivated rocket, stir and serve.

TAGLIOLINI WITH PRAWNS (SHRIMP) AND ZUCCHINI (COURGETTE)

Tagliolini con gamberi e zucchini

30 mL (2 tablespoons) olive oil
2 cloves garlic, minced
1-2 cm (¼-¾ in) cube fresh ginger,
  minced (optional)
500 g (1 lb) small zucchini
  (courgette), finely sliced
300 g (10 oz) green prawns
  (shrimp), shelled
Salt
Black pepper
500 g (1 lb) tagliolini

PRAWNS AND ZUCCHINI prove a winning combination in this favourite 'new' recipe.

Method: Heat the oil, add the garlic (and ginger) and let them begin to change colour before adding the zucchini. As the zucchini begins to soften add the prawns and season to taste. Do not overcook the zucchini. They need to be a good green colour.

The tagliolini will cook in about 3 minutes so have a large pan of salted water ready and cook the pasta while you are seasoning the sauce.

Drain the pasta and stir in the prawns and zucchini.

If the pasta seems a little too dry add a little good quality olive oil. Slimmers can substitute this with a spoonful of the pasta water.

ARTICHOKE RISOTTO

Risotto con carciofi

6 small tender artichokes
Juice of 1 lemon
1 L (1¾ pt) light chicken or
   vegetable stock
50 g (1¾ oz) butter
50 g (1¾ oz) ham (prosciutto crudo
   if available), finely chopped
300 g (10 oz) rice, preferably
   vialone or carnaroli
Parsley, chopped
Salt
Black pepper
50 g (1¾ oz) freshly grated
   Parmesan cheese

FOR THIS RECIPE use only tender young artichokes or small frozen, trimmed artichokes.

Method: Remove the tough outer leaves from the artichokes and cut off the spiky tops. Cut the artichokes into thin vertical slices and put immediately into cold water and lemon juice to prevent them turning brown.

Heat the stock.

Melt the butter and gently fry the ham. After a few minutes put in the artichokes and pour in a little stock. Cover and cook gently for 10 minutes by which time the liquid will have evaporated. Now stir in the rice, using a wooden spoon, and start to add a little stock at a time, waiting for the first liquid to be absorbed before adding more. When the rice is barely cooked sprinkle in the parsley and correct the seasoning. Turn off the heat, stir in the cheese and serve at once.

BAKED PASTA STUFFED WITH WALNUTS AND CHEESE

Lumaconi con noci e gorgonzola e mascarpone

*500 g (1 lb) lumaconi or any large
   pasta suitable for stuffing*
Salt
100 g (3½ oz) shelled walnuts
*100 g (3½ oz) ricotta or cream
   cheese*
*400 g (14 oz) gorgonzola and
   mascarpone, already combined
   or bought separately and
   combined*
200 mL (7 fl oz) cream
*50 g (1¾ oz) freshly grated
   Parmesan cheese*
Black pepper

WALNUTS, CREAMY mascarpone and gorgonzola make a sumptuous filling for large pasta shapes.

Method: Cook the pasta in boiling salted water for *half* the time stated on the packet so that the shapes are pliable but not soft. In a food processor chop the walnuts and process with the ricotta (or cream cheese) and 300 g (10 oz) of gorgonzola and mascarpone.

Stuff the large pasta with this mixture and arrange in an ovenproof dish, lightly coated with a little sauce made by mixing the remaining gorgonzola and mascarpone into the cream. Pour the rest of the sauce over the pasta and sprinkle with Parmesan cheese and black pepper. Bake in a hot oven, 200°C (400°F), until golden brown. Serve at once.

LASAGNE PRIMAVERA

12 sheets white lasagne
1 L (1¾ pt) thin bechamel sauce
(see Cupola of Pancakes,
page 25)
20 basil leaves
18 spears green asparagus
500 g (1 lb) small, tender zucchini
(courgette), cut into thin discs
200 g (7 oz) shelled peas or very
small broad beans
200 g (7 oz) thin green beans
100 g (3½ oz) freshly grated
Parmesan cheese
Black pepper
Salt
1 small fresh mozzarella cheese,
thinly sliced
Butter

I LOVE TO MAKE this pasta dish when the first spring vegetables appear in the market, and my own personal touch is to flavour the bechamel sauce with fragrant basil.

Method: Cook the pasta sheets 2 at a time in a large pan of boiling salted water, to which you have added a little olive oil to prevent the pasta sheets sticking together. After a few minutes lift out the pasta with a slotted spoon and plunge into a bowl of cold water. Remove from the cold water and spread out on kitchen towels to dry. Do not put the sheets on top of each other or they will stick together.

Make a thin bechamel and process with the basil leaves to create a smooth, pale green sauce.

Cook the vegetables separately so that they remain slightly underdone. If you use broad beans remove the outer skin so that they are bright green.

Butter a rectangular ovenproof dish and coat with a thin layer of sauce. Line with three slightly overlapping pasta sheets, and arrange a sprinkling of vegetables over the sheets. Dust with a little Parmesan, black pepper and salt, and then add a little sauce. Build up the layers in this way, reserving some good-looking vegetables for decoration.

The final pasta sheets should be dotted with thin slices of mozzarella then decorated with a regular pattern of vegetables. Add a light sprinkling of Parmesan cheese and dot with a little butter.

Bake in a hot oven, 200°C (400°F), for about 20 minutes.

FRIED PASTRY PATTIES

Panzarotti

100 g (3½ oz) butter
250 g (9 oz) flour, sifted
Salt
1 egg yolk

FILLING

1 tablespoon chopped parsley
70 g (2½ oz) cooked ham, diced
120 g (4 oz) mozzarella, diced
50 g (1¾ oz) freshly grated
    Parmesan cheese
2 eggs, beaten

(If you wish to substitute chopped
    tomatoes for the ham, use only
    1 egg.)

Oil for deep frying
1 beaten egg, to brush over the
    patties before frying

VARIATIONS OF THESE patties are found all over Puglia and Campania.

Method: Rub the butter into the flour and salt then add the egg yolk and a little cold water to make a ball of pastry. Leave the pastry to rest in the refrigerator for at least 30 minutes.

To make the filling, mix together the parsley, ham, mozzarella, Parmesan and beaten eggs.

Roll out the pastry and cut into circles about 8 cm (3 in) diameter using a fluted cutter if possible. Spoon a little filling into the middle of each circle and fold over to form a half moon. Use a little of the beaten egg to seal the edges.

When you are ready to eat, brush patties with beaten egg, heat the oil and fry the patties 2 or 3 at a time until they are golden brown. Drain well on kitchen paper and serve at once.

THIN PASTA SALAD WITH CAVIARE

Insalata di spaghettini e caviale

*100 g (3½ oz) spaghettini or very
    thin pasta*
*15 mL (1 tablespoon) extra virgin
    olive oil*
Juice of 1 lemon
4 teaspoons chopped chives
*1 tablespoon black caviare or
    lumpfish*
*1 tablespoon salmon eggs or red
    lumpfish*

I HAD NEVER UNDERSTOOD the appeal of pasta that
isn't hot but when I was served this at Recco's
Manuelina restaurant I was immediately converted. I
think the secret is the minute portion, served as an
appetiser, which leaves the palate titillated.

The quantities given are for a very small serving.
Increase the quantities if you want a normal starter.

Method: Cook the pasta in boiling salted water,
taking care not to overcook. Drain and season with
olive oil, lemon juice and chives.

Arrange the pasta in a small coil on individual
plates with the dark caviare spooned on top in the
middle, and the red salmon eggs or lumpfish
scattered around this.

PASTA SNAILS STUFFED WITH ZUCCHINI (COURGETTE)

Lumaconi con zucchini e mozzarella

1 kg (2 lb) small zucchini
  (courgette)
30 mL (2 tablespoons) olive oil
Salt
Black pepper
10 marrow flowers, if available
200 g (7 oz) mozzarella, diced
Milk
30 g (1 oz) butter
40 g (1½ oz) plain flour
50 g (1¾ oz) freshly grated
  Parmesan cheese
500 g (1 lb) lumaconi or any large
  pasta suitable for stuffing

IF YOU CAN FIND some marrow flowers, the streaks of orange make this dish look very exotic and it tastes out of this world! It is good for dinner parties because it can be prepared in advance and baked when the guests are ready.

Method: Choose 2 or 3 small zucchini and slice into fine rings. Heat the oil and gently cook the zucchini rings with a little salt and pepper, covering the pan so that they do not brown. If you have marrow flowers remove the stamens and pistils and tear to pieces. They should be cooked for 1 minute with the zucchini rings.

Roughly chop the remaining zucchini and cook quickly in a little boiling salted water, taking care not to overcook and spoil their colour. Drain and purée the zucchini.

Stir half the purée into the pan containing the zucchini rings and heat gently, adding the diced mozzarella.

The rest of the zucchini purée should be diluted with milk to make about 300 mL (10 fl oz) of liquid.

Melt the butter and gently cook the flour, gradually adding the zucchini liquid in the same way as you make a bechamel sauce. Stir in half the Parmesan and season to taste.

Cook the pasta for *half* the time stated on the packet so that the shapes are pliable but not soft. Drain and cool enough to be able to handle. Using a teaspoon put a little filling into each shape and arrange in a single layer in a shallow ovenproof dish over a thin coating of sauce. Pour the remaining sauce evenly over the pasta and sprinkle with the rest of the Parmesan. Add a little black pepper and bake in a hot oven, 220°C (425°F), for 15-20 minutes.

LEEK AND RICE BROTH

Minestra di porri e riso

100 g (3½ oz) butter
300 g (10 oz) leeks, cleaned and cut
   into rings
1 thin rasher streaky bacon
   (optional), chopped
1 clove garlic, minced
1 bay leaf
150 g (5 oz) peeled, chopped potato
Salt
Black pepper
300 g (10 oz) rice, preferably
   arborio or vialone
Nutmeg
75 g (2½ oz) gruyère cheese, diced
75 g (2½ oz) fontina cheese, diced

THE PIEDMONT TOWN of Asti is today associated with sparkling wine, white truffles and great gastronomic delights, but at one time the local produce was almost exclusively garlic and leeks. This recipe was a firm local favourite in the Middle Ages when it was believed that leeks cleansed the blood. Whatever the medicinal properties, this is a tasty, economical broth that brings instant comfort on misty autumn days.

Method: Melt half the butter in a large pan and add half the leeks together with bacon, garlic and bay leaf. Cover and stew over a low heat for 20 minutes.
   Now add the remaining leeks, the potato and about 1.8 L (3 pt) boiling water. Simmer for 15 minutes, season to taste and stir in the rice. Grate in a little nutmeg. When the rice is cooked, mash the potatoes with a wooden spoon and stir in the cheese and the remaining butter.

GNOCCHI WITH CHEESE
Gnocchi alla bava

1½ kg (3 lb) floury potatoes
300 g (10 oz) plain flour or half buckwheat and half plain flour, sifted
Salt
225 g (7½ oz) fontina valdostana cheese, sliced
120 g (4½ oz) butter and extra butter for greasing dish
Black pepper

ALTHOUGH THE ROMAN gnocchi, served traditionally on Thursdays, do not greatly appeal to me, I love these cheesy potato gnocchi from Piedmont.

Method: Cook the potatoes in their skins, peel while still hot and mash. Avoid using a food processor because it ruins the texture of the potatoes. Stir in the flour and salt and beat until you have an elastic dough. I use an electric beater at this stage. Roll into small cylinders on a floured board and cut into flat discs.

In a shallow, buttered ovenproof dish arrange the gnocchi in 2 layers with slices of cheese in the middle. Put curls of butter over the surface and grind over a dusting of black pepper. Bake until golden brown at 240°C (475°F).

PASTA WITH PEAS AND MINT

Tagliolini alla menta

80 g (3 oz) butter
1 small onion, finely chopped
300 g (10 oz) shelled peas
Salt
Black pepper
10 mint leaves
500 g (1 lb) egg pasta like tagliolini
   or fettuccine
50 g (1¾ oz) freshly grated
   Parmesan cheese

THIS DELICATE PASTA is very simple to make and works well even with frozen peas. However you must have fresh mint.

Method: Melt the butter and add the onion. When the onion begins to become transparent add the peas and season to taste. Cover and cook for about 12 minutes.

Roughly chop the mint leaves, leaving a sprig for decoration.

Cook the pasta, taking care not to overcook. Drain the pasta, stir in the peas, cheese and chopped mint.

PASTA WITH CEPS

Ziti con funghi porcini

500 g (1 lb) mushrooms (ceps)
30 mL (2 tablespoons) olive oil
3 cloves garlic, minced
Mint, chopped
Salt
Black pepper
500 g (1 lb) ziti or rigatoni

THE SILA, IN CALABRIA, is famous for its rugged, natural beauty and its great forest which yields up excellent wild mushrooms. Often, by the side of the road, an impromptu market springs up as the local men meet to sell their excess spoils directly from their cars, and to swap among themselves.

Method: Clean the mushrooms with a damp sponge, taking care not to make them too wet and soggy. Finely slice the mushrooms.

Heat the oil, add the garlic and let it begin to change colour before adding the mushrooms. Cover and simmer for 2 minutes then add the mint. Season to taste.

Cook the pasta in a large pan of boiling salted water, taking care not to overcook. Drain, stir in the mushrooms and serve at once.

RAVIOLI WITH FISH AND SHELLFISH

Ravioli di pesce ai frutti di mare

FILLING

*2 skate each weighing about 1 kg
   (2 lb), cleaned and filletted
Fish stock made by boiling together
   500 mL (16 fl oz) salted water,
   1 carrot, 1 onion, 1 stick celery,
   500 mL (16 fl oz) dry white
   wine and any left over fish or
   fish heads*

PASTA

*3 eggs
300 g (10 oz) plain flour*

SAUCE

*30 mL (2 tablespoons) olive oil
3 cloves garlic, minced
2 cuttlefish with the ink sac intact
   (to colour the pasta), cut into
   fine strips
2 small rock octopus, cut into fine
   strips
200 mL (7 fl oz) dry white wine
1 small can Italian tomatoes,
   drained and chopped
1 kg (2 lb) prawns (shrimp),
   shelled
20 mussels
Salt
Pepper*

THIS IS ONE recipe for stuffed fresh pasta that I cannot resist. Fulvio Pierangelini serves this dish in his elegant Tuscan restaurant in San Vincenzo.

Method: Cook the skate for 20 minutes in stock. Remove the skate from the liquid. Skin, then purée the fillets with the stock vegetables to make the pasta stuffing.

Make the pasta by mixing the eggs into the flour. Knead in the food processor for 5 minutes. If you have an intact ink sac with the cuttlefish you can colour half the pasta black by squeezing in the ink and kneading for an extra minute. Leave the pasta to rest for half an hour, covered by plastic food wrap.

To make the sauce, heat the oil, add the garlic and cook until it turns colour. Remove the garlic and add the cuttlefish and octopus. After a few minutes pour in the white wine and add the tomatoes. Cook for 15 minutes then add the shelled prawns and mussels. Cook for a further 10 minutes then season to taste.

Roll out a quarter of the pasta, leaving the rest covered with plastic food wrap, into a thin rectangular strip about 12 cm (5 in) wide and cut into 2 lengths 6 cm (2½ in) wide. The ravioli are going to be 6 cm (2½ in) square. Place a spoonful of filling at regular intervals, then cover with the second strip of pasta. Cut into squares, sealing the edges with a pasta wheel or the prongs of a fork. Continue until all the filling has been used up. If you have made coloured pasta, make half of the ravioli with black pasta and half with white. They have to be cooked in separate pans.

Cook in a large pan of boiling salted water, drain and serve with the sauce.

CUPOLA OF PANCAKES

Cupola di crêpes Gerard

PANCAKES

250 g (8 oz) plain flour
600 mL (1 pt) milk
4 eggs
40 g (1½ oz) melted butter
Salt

BECHAMEL SAUCE

120 g (4 oz) butter
100 g (3½ oz) flour
1 L (1¾ pt) milk
Nutmeg
Salt

FILLING

250 g (8 oz) button mushrooms
25 g (1 oz) butter
50 mL (3½ tablespoons) medium dry sherry
150 g (5 oz) diced ham
150 g (5 oz) diced gruyère cheese
50 g (1¾ oz) freshly grated Parmesan cheese

THIS IS ANOTHER spectacular Neapolitan dish invented by the chef *monzù* Gerard.

Method: Beat together the pancake ingredients and leave to stand for a few hours. Make the pancakes one at a time and stack in a pile to cool so they will be easier to handle.

Prepare the sauce by melting the butter and cooking the flour before gradually stirring in the warm milk seasoned with nutmeg and salt.

Cook the mushrooms in the butter then pour on the sherry and allow it to evaporate. Chop the mushrooms and mix in a bowl with the ham and cheese.

Butter a shallow round ovenproof dish no more than 1 cm (¼ in) high and put in the first pancake. Smear on a little bechamel sauce with the back of a wooden spoon then spread on some of the ham mixture and a sprinkling of gruyère and Parmesan. Cover with the second pancake and repeat the process. The pancakes will gradually form a mound and you should use the bechamel sauce and wooden spoon to mould the cupola evenly.

Brown in a hot oven, 200°C (400°F), and serve at once, cut like a cake in vertical slices. The dish can be prepared in advance and browned at the last minute.

OPEN RAVIOLO

Raviolo aperto

FISH FILLING

180 g (6 oz) butter
200 g (7 oz) green prawns
   (shrimp), shelled and chopped
200 g (7 oz) scallops, removed from
   the shell and chopped
200 g (7 oz) sole fillets
300 mL (10 fl oz) dry white wine
150 mL (5 fl oz) cream
Saffron threads
Salt
White pepper

WHITE PASTA

200 g (7 oz) plain flour
2 eggs

GREEN BASE

100 g (3½ oz) uncooked spinach
200 g (7 oz) plain flour
2 small eggs

6 large flat parsley leaves

GUALTIERO MARCHESI WAS one of the first restaurant owners to introduce a 'new look' in Italian cooking. His open raviolo has become one of the great modern classics and his influence has been far-reaching. Although the raviolo can be made with only white pasta it does look spectacular when prepared with a green base and a large flat parsley leaf pressed between the two layers of the white pasta 'lid'.

Method: Melt the butter and gently cook the shellfish and fish for a few minutes before moistening with the white wine. Cook for another few minutes then remove the shellfish and fish with a slotted spoon.

Put the cream and saffron into the cooking liquid and let it reduce before returning the fish to the sauce. Season to taste.

Make the white pasta dough and leave to rest as in Ravioli with Fish and Shellfish (page 24).

For the green base, wash and cook the spinach, drain very well and purée. The spinach must be very dry before adding to the flour together with the eggs. Prepare in the same way as the white pasta.

Roll out the green base and cut into pieces 10 x 8 cm (4 x 3 in), 1 for each portion.

Roll out the white pasta and for every portion cut out 2 rectangles 10 x 8 cm (4 x 3 in). Arrange a washed and dried parsley leaf in the middle of 1 piece and press a second piece on top. Use the rolling pin to bond the 2 sheets together and trim the now decorated top to measure 10 x 8 cm (4 x 3 in).

Cook the sheets in boiling salted water and drain.

For every portion put a green base on an individual plate, spoon on a portion of fish filling and place the decorated sheet on top. Serve at once.

POTATO CROQUETTES

Crocchè

600 g (1¼ lb) potatoes, boiled in
   their skins
35 g (1¼ oz) butter
1 egg plus one extra yolk, reserve
   the white
50 g (1¾ oz) freshly grated
   Parmesan cheese
Parsley, chopped
Salt
Black pepper
1 egg beaten, plus the remaining
   egg white
Plain flour
Fresh breadcrumbs
Oil for deep frying

THESE CRISP CYLINDERS of fried mashed potatoes belong to the Neapolitan *cucina povera* tradition of *frienno magnanno* (see Yeast Batter, page 39). They are sometimes known as *panzarotti,* but this name is usually reserved for the Fried Pastry Patties, page 17.

The secret of success with this recipe is to work as quickly as possible, mixing in the other ingredients while the potatoes are still hot. This is one occasion where a food processor is not suitable because it makes the mixture too glutinous.

Method: Drain the potatoes and remove the peel as soon as you can handle them. Mash using a potato masher and gradually incorporate the butter, egg and extra yolk, cheese, parsley, salt and pepper. If you wish you can also add any diced ham or salami if you have some at hand.

Shape the mixture with your hands into smooth oblongs.

Whip the remaining egg white and stir it into the beaten egg. Roll the croquettes in the flour then dip them into the egg. Give them a final coating of breadcrumbs before frying them in the hot oil.

SPINACH AND RICOTTA DUMPLINGS

Strozzapreti ('choke the priest')

500 g (1 lb) spinach
100 g (3½ oz) fresh basil, if
    available
350 g (12 oz) ricotta cheese
50 g (1¾ oz) freshly grated
    Parmesan cheese
3 eggs
3 tablespoons white flour
1 teaspoon nutmeg
Salt
Black pepper
Tomato sauce (see Aubergine
    (Eggplant) Timbales with
    Tomato and Basil Sauce,
    page 49)

IN THE PAST many poor villagers regretted the local priest's hearty appetite when he came to call and all over Italy there are mouth-watering regional pasta dishes called 'choke (or strangle) the priest.'

Method: Cook the spinach quickly so that it retains its bright green. Add the basil leaves for the last 30 seconds before draining the spinach. Stand under cold running water then press out all the moisture. Process the dried spinach with the other ingredients then put the mixture in the refrigerator for an hour.

Using a forcing (pastry) bag, squeeze out long cylinders and cut into lengths of 3 cm (1 in). When they are all ready drop them into a large pan of boiling salted water. They are cooked as soon as they float to the top. Remove with a slotted spoon so that they do not break and serve very hot on individual plates containing a little warm tomato sauce.

GREEN HERB RISOTTO

Risotto alle erbe

30 mL (2 tablespoons) olive oil
4 cloves garlic, finely chopped
1 small onion, finely chopped
450 g (15 oz) carnaroli rice
2 small zucchini (courgette)
100 g (3½ oz) spinach
4 cm (1½ in) stick celery
*50 g (1¾ oz) mixed mint, sage and
    rosemary*
*30 g (1 oz) each basil, parsley and
    rocket*
Light stock (salted)
*50 g (1¾ oz) freshly grated
    Parmesan cheese*
30 g (1 oz) butter
Black pepper

I FIRST ATE THIS delicate risotto in Venice. As is appropriate in a city built on water, Venetians serve their risotto slightly liquid — *all' onda* where the rice ripples like a wave if the plate is tilted.

Method: Heat the oil and add the garlic and onion. When they are soft stir in the raw rice and cook, stirring for 5 minutes so that the rice absorbs the oil.

Now add the rest of the vegetables and herbs, all finely chopped, and gradually add the hot stock, a spoonful at a time, as the rice absorbs the liquid. This process will take about 20 minutes. When the rice is cooked, stir in the cheese, dot with butter and add a little freshly ground black pepper, and serve at once.

ASPARAGUS RISOTTO

Risotto con asparagi

1 kg (2 lb) green asparagus
Salt
50 g (1¾ oz) butter
1 medium onion, finely chopped
300 g (10 oz) rice, preferably
    vialone or carnaroli
½ glass dry white wine
A little light stock if necessary
50 g (1¾ oz) freshly grated
    Parmesan cheese
Black pepper

THIS DELICATE, CREAMY, green risotto is one of my favourites and during the asparagus season it can be enjoyed at Emilio Baldi's Venetian restaurant, Antico Martini.

Method: Cut off the extreme tips, 2-3 cm (1-1¼ in) of the asparagus and reserve. Cut the remaining stalks into 4 cm (1¾ in) lengths and cook quickly in a little lightly salted water. When they are tender, purée and sieve to eliminate any tough fibres. Stir this pulp into the cooking liquid to make an asparagus stock.

Melt 40 g (1½ oz) of the butter in a large pan, add the onion and let it begin to soften before adding the asparagus tips. With a wooden spoon stir in the rice and let it absorb the flavour of the butter and onions before pouring over the wine. Turn up the heat so that the wine evaporates quickly then ladle on a little boiling asparagus stock. When the rice has absorbed the liquid add another ladle of stock and continue in this way until the rice is cooked. You may need to use a different stock if the asparagus stock is finished before the rice is tender. It is most important to add only boiling stock a little at a time to the rice. This process usually takes about 20 minutes and needs constant care.

When the rice is cooked check for seasoning and stir in the remaining butter and Parmesan cheese. I usually like to add some freshly ground black pepper.

RICE AND PEAS

Risi e bisi

40 g (1½ oz) butter
1 small onion, finely chopped
2 thin rashers bacon, chopped
  (optional)
Parsley, chopped
400 g (14 oz) shelled peas
1 L (1¾ pt) light stock
250 g (8 oz) rice, preferably vialone
  or carnaroli
50 g (1¾ oz) freshly grated
  Parmesan cheese
Salt
Black pepper

THIS VENETIAN SPECIALITY is traditionally made with the very first sweet young peas. However, it can be made successfully with frozen peas if a well-flavoured stock is used. If you do have fresh young peas cook the washed empty pods in some lightly salted boiling water to make the stock. This dish is meant to be more liquid than a risotto so that it resembles a dense broth.

Method: Melt half the butter in a large pan and add the onion, bacon and parsley. After a few minutes add the peas and 2 full ladles of boiling water. If the peas are not young and sweet add a pinch of sugar. Cover and cook for 5 minutes or a little longer if the peas are rather large.

Add the boiling stock and the rice. Do not cover. It can be stirred occasionally and will usually take about twenty minutes to cook over medium heat. Like pasta, you should try the rice, so that it is cooked to your own taste.

When the rice is cooked stir in the remaining butter and the freshly grated cheese. Check the seasoning and grind a little black pepper on top.

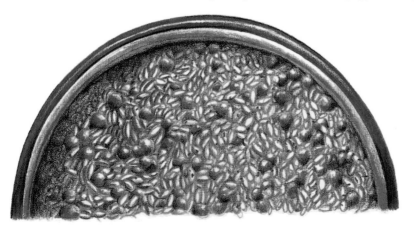

PASTA WITH SARDINES

Pasta siciliana con le sarde

750 g (1½ lb) fresh small sardines
500 g (1 lb) wild fennel
45 mL (3 tablespoons) olive oil
1 large onion, finely sliced
5 salted anchovies or 10 fillets,
    chopped
⅛ teaspoon or a generous pinch of
    saffron
50 g (1¾ oz) sultanas, soaked in a
    little warm water
50 g (1¾ oz) pine nuts
Salt
Black pepper
500 g (1 lb) bucatini
50 g (1¾ oz) almonds, peeled,
    toasted and roughly chopped

THIS DISH IS ONE of the great glories of the Sicilian *cucina povera*. It is really a one-course feast! If you cannot find wild fennel use the feathery tops and tubes of fennel bulbs.

Method: Clean the sardines, removing the guts, head and back bone. Do not divide into 2, however.

Clean and chop the fennel, then cook in abundant boiling salted water that will later be used to cook the pasta. Drain the fennel and chop finely in a food processor.

Heat half the oil and gently cook the onion until it is soft. Add half the sardines, choosing the more mangled-looking fish. Cook for 5 minutes then add the anchovy, pushing with a wooden spoon until it has melted. Now add the fennel, saffron, drained sultanas, pine nuts, salt and pepper. Process this mixture to make a coarse sauce.

Heat the rest of the oil in a second pan and gently cook the remaining sardines on both sides, taking care not to break them. Season to taste.

Heat the fennel water, adding more salted water if necessary, and cook the pasta for *half* the time stated on the packet. Drain the pasta and arrange a thin layer in an ovenproof dish.

Cover the pasta with half the sauce then make a second layer of pasta. Pour over the remaining sauce and then make a final layer of pasta. Arrange the whole sardines on top of the pasta and sprinkle with the almonds.

Bake in the oven, 150°C (300°F), for 20 minutes.

SPINACH AND RICE TART

Torta verde

60 g (2 oz) butter
3 leeks, cut into thin rings
2 cloves garlic, finely chopped
50 g (1¾ oz) streaky bacon, finely chopped
1 kg (2 lb) spinach, roughly chopped
Salt
Black pepper
150 g (5 oz) rice, preferably arborio
Light stock
4 eggs, beaten
30 g (1 oz) freshly grated Parmesan cheese
Nutmeg
Fresh breadcrumbs
30 g (1 oz) butter for the topping

SPINACH, RICE AND cheese go beautifully together in this recipe from Piedmont, but any leafy vegetable can be used.

Method: In a large pan or wok melt half the butter and add the leeks. Cover and stew gently until they are soft then add the garlic and bacon. When the garlic begins to turn colour add the spinach and a little salt and pepper. Cook gently and when the spinach is reduced stir in the rice and a ladle of boiling stock. Add a ladle of stock from time to time until the rice is cooked. All the liquid must be absorbed but the rice must remain firm, so you need to be sparing with the stock.

Remove from the heat and stir in the eggs, cheese and nutmeg. Butter a flat, round oven dish and dust with breadcrumbs. Spoon in the spinach mixture, levelling off the top. Sprinkle with more breadcrumbs and dot with the remaining butter. Bake in a moderate oven, 170°C (325°F), for about 1 hour.

EASTER PASTA

Pasta fresca per Pasqua

1 kg (2 lb) spinach
4 eggs
400 g (14 oz) plain flour
Salt
Nutmeg
6 very fresh farm eggs
Black pepper
200 g (7 oz) butter
50 g (1¾ oz) freshly grated
   Parmesan cheese

USING FRESH PASTA it is possible to make pasta to suit any occasion. In Piacenza, the Antico Teatro restaurant have made a bird-shaped template from stiff board and at Easter they serve a pasta bird with rosemary twig legs, stuffed with spinach and an egg. The fresh pasta takes the same time to cook as the egg white and so the yolk remains runny. I have given the quantity for 6 but in order to serve with the yolk still runny to 6 people I think you would need to cook and serve 2 at a time. I have only ever prepared for 2.

Method: Wash the spinach and cook quickly in the water remaining on the leaves. Drain well and chop finely.

Make the pasta dough with the eggs and flour and leave to rest in the same way as in the recipe for Ravioli with Fish and Shellfish, page 24.

Roll out thinly, big enough to cut out 12 pasta shapes, and cut into the desired shape using a template. On the bottom layer arrange a small amount of chopped spinach seasoned with a little salt and nutmeg. Make a hollow in the spinach and break in a small egg. Season with salt and pepper. Carefully cover with the top layer to avoid breaking the yolk. Seal the edges well with a smooth pastry wheel or a spoon handle. Gently lower into a pan of boiling salted water using a fish slice. Remove after 3 minutes and pour on a little melted butter and a sprinkling of Parmesan. Serve at once.

FRIED RICE CROQUETTES STUFFED WITH MOZZARELLA

Suppli

*400 g (14 oz) rice, preferably
    risotto*
Salt
100 g (3½ oz) butter
*150 g (5 oz) freshly grated
    Parmesan cheese*
2 eggs, beaten
Black pepper
100 g (3½ oz) ham or salami, diced
300 g (10 oz) mozzarella, diced
*Plain flour, 2 eggs, beaten and
    fresh breadcrumbs to coat the
    croquettes*
Oil for deep frying

THESE CRUNCHY RICE croquettes are sold all over Rome as a quick, hot snack. As they are eaten, the mozzarella cheese in the middle pulls out, looking rather like telephone cables, which gives them their Italian name. They can be made with a tomato and chicken liver filling but I prefer the version using ham and cheese. This recipe will make 18 croquettes.

Method: Cook the rice in boiling salted water, drain and while it is still hot stir in the butter, cheese, eggs and black pepper. Allow to cool.

When the rice is cool divide into balls and make a hole with your thumb. Fill this hole with the ham and cheese cubes then form a smooth slightly elongated croquette.

Dust with flour, roll in egg then breadcrumbs and deep fry until golden brown.

PIZZA

PIZZA BASE

25 g (1 oz) fresh yeast
Tepid water
1 teaspoon salt
15 mL (1 tablespoon) olive oil
500 g (4 cups) plain flour

ALTHOUGH DEEP PIZZAS have their fans my love is reserved for the thin, crisp sheets of *pizza rustica* which are baked in great black trays and sold by the slice all over Rome. My all-time favourite toppings are potato slices sprinkled with rosemary, and discs of zucchini (courgette) and mozzarella.

I often make crisp discs about 6 cm (2½ in) in diameter topped with zucchini (courgette) for pre-dinner nibbles. The quantities given are for full-size pizzas. Halve the quantities to make *pizette* (tiny pizzas).

Method: Dissolve the yeast in a little tepid water then add the salt and oil. Put the flour in a bowl or a food processor and pour in the yeast mixture. Gradually add enough tepid water to make a stiff bread dough and work until it is smooth and elastic. Cover with plastic food wrap or, better still, put the dough in a large, oiled plastic bag. Leave in a warm place for about 45 minutes to rise. Divide into 6 balls and roll out to make thin discs.

POTATO TOPPING: Boil the potatoes in their skins until they are just cooked. Peel and cut into thin slices which should be arranged slightly overlapping over the pizza base. Sprinkle generously with rosemary and season with salt and lots of black pepper. Dribble over a little olive oil and bake in a hot oven, 250°C (475°F), for 15 minutes.

ZUCCHINI (COURGETTE) TOPPING: Gently fry thin slices of zucchini in a little olive oil. Season with salt and black pepper and arrange in overlapping slices on the pizza base. Arrange 4 or 5 thin slices of mozzarella on the top of the zucchini and sprinkle a little freshly grated Parmesan cheese on top. Again, bake in a hot oven, 250°C (475°F), for 15 minutes.

FOCACCIA WITH CHEESE

Focaccia di Manuelina

Tepid water
400 g (14 oz) plain flour
Salt
15 mL (1 tablespoon) olive oil
400 g (14 oz) soft creamy cheese
  like strachinella

AT THE END of the last century in the Ligurian town of Recco, a local girl, Manuelina, invented a delicious thin pastry crust with cheese in the middle. Her fame spread and soon fashionable Ligurians started to arrive in coachloads from Genoa to round off an evening at the opera or theatre with a feast of hot crisp *focaccia*. Even today the Manuelina restaurant serves the same treat but it can easily be prepared at home.

Method: Add enough tepid water to the flour and salt to make a soft dough. Knead for a few minutes then leave to rest for an hour, covered by an inverted pudding basin.

Roll out thinly and cut 2 circles 28 cm (11 in) in diameter. Oil a baking tray and place 1 pastry circle, on the tray. Spread evenly with cheese then cover with the second circle, moistening the outer edge to get a better seal. Cook in a hot oven, 230°C (450°F), for 20 minutes. Serve at once.

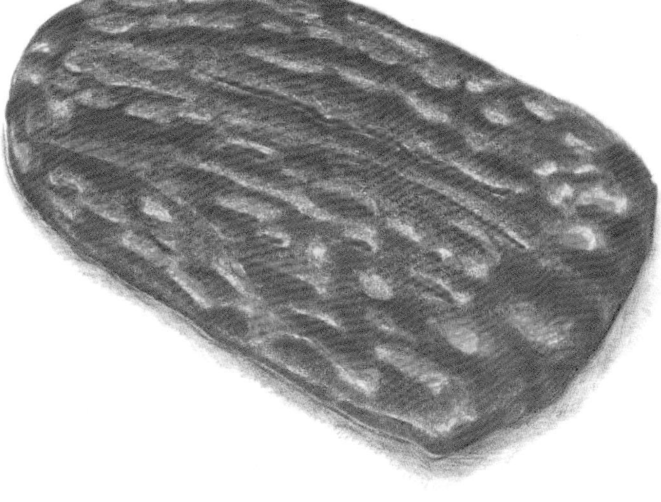

LITTLE GORGONZOLA PASTRIES

Pizzette al gorgonzola

60 g (2 oz) butter
125 g (4 oz) gorgonzola cheese
2 egg yolks
200 g (7 oz) plain flour
Nutmeg
Black pepper
Salt
Egg white, beaten

I LIKE TO SERVE these little *pizzette* as cocktail nibbles but they work equally well if made slightly larger and stuffed with a savoury filling like cooked spinach or mushrooms.

Method: Process the butter, cheese and egg yolks, and gradually add the flour to make a smooth dough. Season to taste. Leave the dough to rest in the refrigerator for about 40 minutes, then roll out thinly and cut into 5 cm (2 in) rings with a fluted pastry cutter. Brush the top with a little beaten egg white and bake in a hot oven, 200°C (400°F), until golden brown.

YEAST BATTER

Pasta cresciuta

25 g (1 oz) fresh yeast
250 mL (8 fl oz) tepid water
300 g (10 oz) plain flour, sifted
Salt

SUGGESTED FILLINGS

*Marrow flowers with the stalk,
stamens and pistils removed.
The flower is carefully opened
and small pieces of mozzarella
and anchovy fillet inserted
inside.*

*Young artichokes cut into quarters
with the tough leaves and
'choke' removed.*

*Zucchini (courgette) and aubergine
(eggplant) cut into thick sticks
or rings.*

IN NAPLES AT ONE time, every neighbourhood had its *friggitoria* — humble ingredients transformed into crisp morsels of temptation by their coating of fluffy yeast batter. Glass cases set out in the street proudly displayed samples of the treats to be enjoyed and the only limit was set by the cook's imagination.

These golden delights must be enjoyed the moment they emerge from the sizzling oil so, at home, the tradition of *frienno magnanno* — eating while frying — evolved. The women snacked standing over the hot oil, while the men sat back to enjoy a constantly replenished supply of *pizzelle* and *fritelle*.

Method: Crumble the yeast into a little tepid water and mix to a smooth cream. Add about ⅔ of the remaining tepid water and stir into the flour and salt. Cover with a cloth and put in a warm place to rise for about 1–1½ hours.

When you are ready to use the batter check its consistency. Add a little more tepid water if the batter seems too thick but remember it needs to be fairly dense so that it clings to the vegetables.

FRITELLE: *Fritelle* are made with the same recipe using much less water. The ingredients are stirred into the thick batter and spoonfuls of the mixture are dropped into the hot oil. In the south of Italy *cecenielli* — newborn fish — are cooked in this way, but I like to use a combination of chopped spring onions and mussels. Diced zucchini (courgette), potatoes and mozzarella make another tasty filling and it is fun to experiment making new cocktail nibbles.

VEGETABLES

VEGETABLES

DURING THE RENAISSANCE, Lorenzo the Magnificent's emissary to Naples described the people there as *mangiafoglie,* leaf-eaters, and the term could equally well have been applied to other poor regions and all people of the south. Even today when the standard of living is generally high, this vegetarian tradition endures and I don't think an Italian could survive without a daily supply of fresh vegetables.

Frozen food manufacturers have made little headway in Italy where the street markets woo their daily customers with the excellence of their produce. The stall holders wash the mud off their spinach and broccoli and remove the tough stalks before arranging them in glistening green piles. Trimmed artichokes bob about in pails of acidulated water and judiciously selected chopped vegetables form bright pyramids of temptation. Baskets of crisp mixed salad contain at least six different green leaves enlivened by the fragments of purple radicchio.

The sunny climate and mineral-enriched volcanic soil impart a unique flavour to Italian peppers, artichokes and aubergines (eggplants) and the incomparable Neapolitan tomatoes, in particular, owe their richly deserved fame to the outpourings of Vesuvius.

Since Roman times people have lived off their kitchen gardens. The countryside is teeming with uncultivated bounty such as *cicoria di campo,* or wild batavia, wild rocket and the tiny field asparagus which has become a much sought-after luxury item. Today few people have the time or inclination to search for these hidden treasures, but many still maintain their own kitchen gardens.

In the past, vegetables, pulses and bread or pasta provided

a complete meal for many families. Ingenious recipes evolved to provide some variety in the daily fare. As evidence of the important role vegetables still play in Italian cooking, they are regarded as a course in their own right, not a garnish, and they are always served on a separate plate.

CARDOONS BAKED WITH PARMESAN CHEESE
Cardi alla Parmigiana

1 kg (2 lb) cardoons
Salt
1 lemon, cut in half
1 tablespoon plain flour
100 g (3½ oz) freshly grated
    Parmesan cheese
100 g (3½ oz) butter
Black pepper

CARDOONS, LIKE THE artichoke, belong to the thistle family and they are grown around the Mediterranean for their long stringy stalks. When they are cut they must be rubbed with lemon or put into acidulated water to prevent them turning brown. The stringy fibres need to be removed but with the following recipe this can be done more easily after the initial cooking period.

Method: Wash the cardoons, cut them into 4 cm (1½ in) lengths and cook in boiling salted water to which you have added the lemon and flour to keep the vegetable a good colour. Cook for about 40 minutes until tender then plunge into cold water. At this stage the tough fibres will peel away easily.

Butter an oval ovenproof dish and make a layer of cardoons, topped with half the cheese and butter. Make a second layer covered with the remaining butter and cheese. Grind on a little black pepper and bake in a moderately hot oven, 180°C (350°F), for about 30 minutes.

SWEET YELLOW PEPPERS WITH ANCHOVY SAUCE

Bagna cauda per l' estate di La Contea

6 sweet yellow peppers
6 cloves garlic
Anchovy fillets, weighing the same
*   as the garlic cloves*
90 mL (3 fl oz) olive oil
Chopped herbs including parsley,
*   chives, marjoram and basil*
Black pepper
Salt, if necessary

PIEDMONT IS FAMOUS for its Bagna Cauda — sticks of various vegetables dipped in a hot, buttery anchovy sauce simmering over a small flame. Claudia and Tonino Verro serve this summer version at La Contea restaurant in Neive.

Method: Roast the peppers over a naked flame or under a grill until their skin blisters and peels off easily. Remove the seeds and divide into uniform strips.

   Process all the other ingredients, except salt, to make a smooth sauce. Check to see if any salt is needed then pour mixture over the pepper fillets.

STUFFED PEPPER FILLETS

Involtini di peperoni

200 g (7 oz) canned tuna in olive oil
2 tablespoons creamed horseradish
3 large red peppers

THIS IS A LIGHT starter belonging to the new school of Italian cooking.

Method: Purée the tuna with the creamed horseradish to make a smooth paste.

Roast the peppers over a naked flame, under or over a very hot grill or in the oven until the skin blisters. Peel off the skin and divide into fillets about 4 cm (1½ in) wide. Coat each fillet with a thick layer of the tuna paste and roll into neat cylinders. Arrange on a serving plate with the seam downwards.

GREEN ASPARAGUS WITH EGGS

Asparagi alla Milanese

2 kg (4 lb) green asparagus
6 eggs
100 g (3½ oz) butter
Salt
75 g (2½ oz) freshly grated
    Parmesan cheese
Black pepper

THESE QUANTITIES are enough for 6 people as a main dish.

Method: Wash the asparagus, break off and discard the tough ends and steam quickly until they are tender.

Fry the eggs very gently in half the butter. Do not let the whites get crisp. Arrange the drained asparagus on a serving dish, add a little salt and cover with the Parmesan, pepper and remaining melted butter. Place the eggs on top when they are still so hot that the cheese begins to melt. Serve at once.

BAKED SICILIAN AUBERGINES (EGGPLANTS)

Melanzane alla Siciliana

4 large aubergines (eggplants)
Salt
Plain flour
2 eggs, beaten
60 mL (4 tablespoons) olive oil
Black pepper
2 tablespoons chopped oregano
250 g (9 oz) mozzarella cheese, cut
*   into thin slices*
Tomato sauce (see Aubergine
*   (Eggplant) Timbales with*
*   Tomato and Basil Sauce,*
*   page 49)*

SICILY MAKES MASTERLY use of the aubergine which was first brought to Italy by Saracen invaders. Initially aubergines were believed to be poisonous, but the Carmelite monks, who had grown familiar with them during their Crusading days, served them in their refectories to no ill effect and they soon became a popular vegetable in southern Italy.

Variations of this dish are found all over Italy but this version uses no Parmesan cheese and the tomato sauce is served separately. Aubergines inevitably absorb a lot of oil when they are fried. Slimmers might prefer to wrap the sliced aubergines in aluminium foil and cook without oil for 15 minutes in the oven instead of the preliminary frying.

Method: Cut the aubergines into ½ cm (¼ in) thick slices, cover with salt and leave for at least an hour to purge their bitter juices. Wash and dry the slices before dipping them in the flour and the beaten eggs. Fry a few slices at a time in hot oil and when they are golden brown put them to drain on kitchen paper.

Oil an oven dish large enough to contain half the aubergine slices in one layer. Season the first layer with salt, pepper and oregano then cover with the mozzarella. Arrange the remaining aubergines over the cheese, season in the same way and brush with a little olive oil.

Bake in a pre-heated oven, 170°C (325°F), for 15 minutes. Serve in wedges accompanied by a little tomato sauce.

AUBERGINE (EGGPLANT) TIMBALES WITH TOMATO AND BASIL SAUCE

Sformatino di melanzane

1 kg (2 lb) aubergines (eggplants), peeled and cut into strips, except for some cut into 6 uniform slices to be fried and kept aside as a base for the turned-out timbales
Salt
60 mL (4 tablespoons) olive oil
2 cloves garlic, crushed
3 eggs
70 g (2¼ oz) freshly grated Parmesan cheese
Pepper

TOMATO AND BASIL SAUCE

15 mL (1 tablespoon) olive oil
1 small onion, chopped
2 cloves garlic, minced
400 g (14 oz) canned Italian plum tomatoes
8 basil leaves

THIS IS A VERY easy starter that always proves popular whatever the season. Vegetarian friends make larger ring moulds as a main course.

Method: Sprinkle the aubergines with salt and leave to drain in a colander to purge the bitter juice.

Heat the oil and gently fry the garlic until it is golden brown. Add the rinsed, dried aubergines and cook until they are soft. Remove and drain on kitchen paper.

Fry the slices to be used as a base until they are golden brown. Set aside on kitchen paper.

Process the aubergine strips with the eggs, cheese and seasoning. Spoon into small, oiled moulds, cover tightly with oiled aluminium foil and cook in a bain-marie in the oven at 180°C (375°F), for about 30 minutes.

To make the sauce, heat the oil and gently fry the onion and garlic until they are transparent. Add the tomatoes and cook quickly in a shallow uncovered pan so that the sauce thickens and remains a bright red. Season to taste then purée with the basil leaves.

When the aubergine timbales are cooked, leave them to stand for about 10 minutes. Turn them out onto the rounds of aubergine placed on individual plates and spoon a little sauce by the side.

ORANGE AND FENNEL SALAD

Insalata di arance e finocchi

3 bulbs of fennel
45 mL (3 tablespoons) extra virgin
*   olive oil*
Salt
Black pepper
6 oranges

PUGLIA GIVES US this unusual salad which can be served as an antipasto, a side dish or even after the main course. In Puglia they often serve a dish of crisp fennel at the end of the meal instead of fruit, and with this recipe you get the best of both worlds.

Method: Remove the tough outer layer and 'core' of the fennel and cut into thin vertical slices. Leave for 10 minutes in the olive oil, salt and pepper.
   Peel the oranges and cut into fine round slices, collecting all the juice that escapes. Drain the liquid from the fennel and process with the orange juice to make a cream.
   Arrange the orange and fennel slices on a plate and dress with the creamy sauce.

TUSCAN BEANS WITH TOMATO AND SAGE

Fagioli all' uccelletto

350 g (12 oz) dried white
    cannellini beans
Salt
100 mL (3½ fl oz) olive oil
3 cloves garlic, minced
1 teaspoon chopped sage
300 g (10 oz) peeled Italian
    tomatoes, fresh or canned

THESE BEANS GET their name from the judicious flavouring of sage and tomatoes which are used in Tuscany when cooking small birds. This recipe can be cooked as a vegetarian treat or served with grilled or roast meat. It goes very well with meaty sausages, too.

Method: Soak the beans for 12 hours in cold water. Bring 2 L (3½ pt) of water to the boil, add a little salt and the drained beans. Bring quickly back to the boil then turn down the heat to minimum and simmer *without stirring* for about 3 hours.

Heat the oil and fry the garlic until it begins to change colour. Add the sage and the drained beans. Stir gently with a wooden spoon to coat every bean with oil, taking care not to break up the beans. Add the tomatoes and simmer gently for another 15 minutes.

This dish can be prepared well in advance of serving and the beans themselves can be cooked the day before if desired.

BAKED POTATO CAKE

Gattò

1 kg (2 lb) potatoes
4 eggs, beaten
50 g (1¾ oz) freshly grated
  Parmesan cheese
150 mL (5 fl oz) milk
Salt
Black pepper
150 g (5 oz) ham or salami, diced
150 g (5 oz) butter
Fresh breadcrumbs
200 g (7 oz) mozzarella cheese,
  sliced
100 g (3½ oz) smoked Provola or
  other available equivalent
  cheese, sliced

FOR CENTURIES NAPLES suffered hardship and deprivation under successive foreign domination and for the ordinary people politics and patriotism became irrelevant in the face of the invincible, omnipresent enemy, hunger. *O Francia o Spagna purchè si magna.* Yet the Neapolitan's joy of life could not be quelled and every simple meal was seen as a victory. Great ingenuity was used to turn homely, inexpensive ingredients into a feast and in this recipe comparatively costly ham, cheese and eggs are made to go a long way with the help of puréed potatoes. The name reveals the French influence, subject to Neapolitan spelling! In the rare event that any *gattò* is left over it can be turned into Potato Croquettes (see page 27).

Method: Boil the potatoes in their skins and when you can bear to handle them remove the skin and mash. Do not use a food processor for this because it makes the potatoes too glutinous.

Stir in the eggs, Parmesan, milk, salt and pepper, then add the ham or salami.

Use a little butter to grease a flat ovenproof dish and dust with breadcrumbs. Spoon in half the potato mixture and level off with the back of the spoon. Arrange the mozzarella and other cheese over this layer then spoon in the remaining potato mixture. Level the surface then scatter over breadcrumbs. Dot with little pieces of the remaining butter and season with black pepper. Bake in a moderate oven for 30 to 45 minutes.

CEPS COOKED ON A VINE LEAF

Funghi porcini su foglie di vite

4 cloves garlic, finely chopped
100 g (3½ oz) streaky bacon, finely chopped
30 mL (2 tablespoons) olive oil
30 mL (2 tablespoons) white wine
6 large ceps (mushroom) heads
Salt
6 grape vine leaves, washed and dried
Parsley, chopped

THIS MAKES A sumptuous first course, or with really big ceps it could be the main dish.

Method: Cook the garlic and bacon in the oil until they begin to change colour. Pour on the wine and add the mushroom heads. Season, cover the pan and cook gently for a few minutes.

Arrange the vine leaves on an oiled baking tray. Put a mushroom in the middle of each leaf and arrange a scattering of bacon and garlic on top. Roast in a pre-heated oven, 180°C (350°F), for 10 minutes. Sprinkle with parsley and serve.

GONZAGA FENNEL SOUP

Minestra di finocchio

8 fennel bulbs
2 L (3½ pt) fresh chicken stock
60 g (2 oz) pine nuts, chopped
5 egg yolks
200 mL (7 fl oz) fresh cream
Juice of 3 lemons
Grated cinnamon

THIS IS ANOTHER subtle, intriguing first course which the Cigno restaurant in Mantova has adapted for modern tastes from the fifteenth century version served at the Gonzaga court.

Method: Cut the fennel into small cubes, removing any tough, discoloured sections. Simmer in boiling stock for about 40 minutes. This part of the recipe can be prepared several hours in advance if required.

Combine the pine nuts, egg yolks, cream and lemon juice and just before serving stir very slowly into the soup which should be hot but not boiling. Check for seasoning and add a little grated cinnamon.

BROCCOLI WITH GARLIC AND CHILLI PEPPER

Broccoletti in padella

1 kg (2 lb) broccoli, turnip tops, or
    cauliflower
45 mL (3 tablespoons) olive oil
1 chilli pepper, whole
3 cloves garlic, minced
Salt

MANY TRATTORIAS IN Rome, for convenience, cook
the vegetables in boiling, salted water, drain them
and then 'pass' the vegetables in a frying pan with
olive oil, garlic and *peperoncino*. This method works
well but the result is much better if you actually cook
the greens in the aromatic oil. Any leafy green
vegetable can be used but my favourite is turnip tops
or cauliflower.

Method: Wash the broccoli or other vegetable,
removing any tough stalks and divide into flowerets
and small leaves.
    I use my wok for this recipe. Heat the oil and add
the whole chilli and the garlic. Stir in the broccoli
and let the oil coat each part. Cover and cook over a
low heat until they are cooked but still crisp. Season
to taste.

ROMAN ARTICHOKES FROM THE OLD GHETTO
Carciofi alla Giudia

6 young, tender artichokes
Lemon
Oil for deep frying
Salt

MANY ROMAN SPECIALITIES were 'stolen' from traditional Jewish cooking, and this simple, delicious recipe is still served in trattorias around the old ghetto area.

Method: Choose young artichokes with little or no 'choke'. Remove the tough outer leaves and any split ends at the points of the leaves. Rub with lemon to prevent them turning black. Open the leaves and push them point down onto a hard surface so that the artichoke opens out like a water lily. Fry them in hot oil until they are brown and crispy. Drain them on kitchen paper, salt lightly and serve at once.

CHESTNUT TIMBALES

Sformato di castagne

500 g (1 lb) chestnuts
1 bay leaf
2 cloves garlic
15 mL (1 tablespoon) olive oil
1 small onion, minced
2 eggs
250 g (8 oz) ricotta cheese
30 g (1 oz) freshly grated
    Parmesan cheese
30 g (1 oz) butter, melted
2 lemons, one with the peel grated,
    the other lemon with its peel in
    threads (use a zester)
Salt
Black pepper

WHEN I AM SERVING beef or turkey I often make these little chestnut moulds which go so well with roast meat or *brasato*.

Method: Make a circular slit in each chestnut then boil them with the bay leaf, garlic and a little olive oil for about 40 minutes. Peel while they are still hot and purée. Leave 2 or 3 whole for decoration. Put the purée in a processor with the onion, eggs, ricotta, Parmesan, melted butter and grated peel. Make a smooth cream and season to taste. Spoon into 6 lightly greased moulds and stand them in a baking tin containing hot water. Bake in a moderately hot oven, 180°C (350°F), for about 35 minutes. Turn out and decorate with some pieces of chestnut and the zested lemon threads.

FRIED FENNEL

Finocchi fritti

6 fennel bulbs
Salt
50 g (1¾ oz) pecorino cheese,
    grated
Parsley, chopped
Fresh breadcrumbs
Black pepper
2 eggs, beaten
Oil for deep frying

FENNEL IS A VERSATILE vegetable that can be used in a myriad of ways. In the south, in Puglia, it is often served raw at the end of the meal to cleanse the palate in place of fruit. The Sicilians combine fennel and tomatoes to make an interesting pasta sauce. Two of my favourite fennel recipes are very simple and make a perfect accompaniment to plain grilled or roast meat, especially pork.

Method: Remove the tough outer leaves and tubes and cut the fennel into thin slices. Lightly cook in boiling salted water until just tender. Drain well.

Mix together the cheese, parsley, breadcrumbs and pepper. Roll each section of fennel in the egg then in the breadcrumb mixture. Just before serving heat the oil and deep fry.

FENNEL BAKED IN THE OVEN

Finocchi al forno

6 fennel bulbs
30 g (1 oz) butter
50 g (1¾ oz) freshly grated
*   Parmesan cheese*
Black pepper

Method: Prepare the fennel as for Fried Fennel (page 58). Butter a shallow ovenproof serving dish and arrange the fennel in a single layer. Sprinkle with the Parmesan and dot with butter. Add black pepper and bake in a hot oven until golden brown.

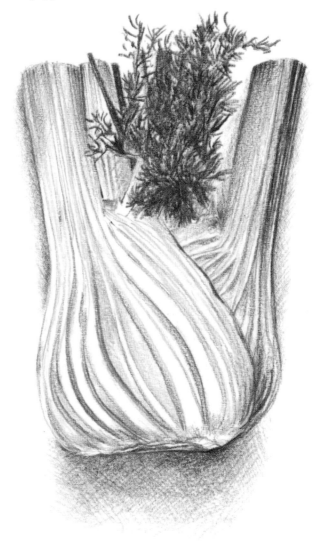

CARROTS WITH MARSALA WINE
Carote al Marsala

750 g (1½ lb) young carrots
75 g (2½ oz) butter
200 mL (7 fl oz) Marsala, or, if not
available, medium dry sherry
Salt
Black pepper

THIS DELICIOUS RECIPE from Sicily transforms the humble carrot.

Method: Slice the carrots into thin discs. Heat the butter and when it begins to foam quickly brown the carrots. Pour on the wine and add a little salt and pepper. Cover and cook slowly until the carrots are tender.

MUSHROOM AND PARMESAN TART

Capriccio di funghi al parmigiano

70 g (2½ oz) potatoes
600 g (1¼ lb) fresh ceps or field
*   mushrooms*
50 g (1¾ oz) butter
200 g (7 oz) freshly grated
*   Parmesan cheese*
Salt
Black pepper
Parsley, chopped
Short crust pastry made in the
*   usual way with 300 g (10 oz)*
*   plain flour and 150 g (5 oz)*
*   butter*
1 egg, beaten

AN ELEGANT FIRST course for a special dinner party, or, served with a good salad, a delicious one-course lunch. If fresh, moist Parmesan cheese is not available it is better to substitute a hard cheese.

Method: Boil the potato in its skin, peel then cut into thin slices. Clean the ceps with a wet sponge and dry well with kitchen paper. Do not let the mushrooms get too wet or they will spoil.

Butter 6 individual flat ovenproof dishes and line with thin flakes of Parmesan. Cover this with a layer of ceps, sliced thinly, salt and pepper. Now make a layer of potato, sprinkled with parsley and seasoned. Make a final layer of mushrooms, season, and add a small knob of butter. Cover with a thin pastry crust, well sealed over the outer rim, glaze with the egg and bake at 180°C (350°F), for 15 minutes.

ARTICHOKE, PEAS AND BROAD BEANS
Vignarola

30 mL (2 tablespoons) olive oil
1 leek, finely chopped
4 artichokes
Mint
Salt
Black pepper
500 g (1 lb) broad beans, shelled
500 g (1 lb) peas, shelled

I HAVE NOT BEEN able to discover the origin of this name, but variations of this dish are found all over Puglia and the south.

Method: Heat the oil and add the leek. Remove the tough leaves from the artichokes and cut into quarters, removing the 'choke'. Add to the oil with the mint, salt and pepper. Cover and stew gently for about 15 minutes. Now add the beans and peas and a little water if necessary. Cook until the vegetables are soft and the liquid has almost disappeared.

BAKED CRUSTY GREENS

Minestra maritata a ru furnu

1 kg (2 lb) mixed green vegetables, such as broccoli, cabbage and batavia (broad-leafed green endive)
Salt
3 slices coarse stale bread made into crumbs
30 mL (2 tablespoons) olive oil
2 cloves garlic, minced

THIS PEASANT DISH from Calabria makes a marvellous, tasty snack and I often serve it with grilled meat.

Method: Cook the vegetables quickly (do not overcook as they will cook further in the oven) in boiling salted water, drain and plunge immediately into cold water to keep them a good green colour. Drain and arrange in an oiled ovenproof dish and cover with breadcrumbs. Heat the oil and add the garlic, letting it turn golden brown. Pour the hot oil and garlic over the breadcrumbs and bake in a hot oven, 200°C (400°F), until the crust is a good brown.

VEGETABLES WITH EGGS

Ciambotta

400 g (14 oz) aubergine (eggplant)
Salt
45 mL (3 tablespoons) olive oil
400 g (14 oz) potatoes, peeled and
    sliced
400 g (14 oz) sweet green peppers,
    cut into rough pieces
500 g (1 lb) ripe red tomatoes or
    canned Italian tomatoes,
    chopped
Black pepper
6 eggs, beaten

THIS IS ANOTHER recipe from Calabria which is one of my favourite supper dishes.

Method: Cut the aubergine into strips and leave sprinkled with salt to purge the bitter juice. Heat the oil and add the potatoes. Add the peppers to the pan. Next put in the chopped tomatoes and the rinsed and dried aubergine. Season and stir the vegetables frequently while they are cooking. This part of the recipe can be prepared in advance if required. Before serving, heat and stir in the eggs and let them set.

MINESTRONE SOUP WITH PESTO

Minestrone col pesto

*150 g (5 oz) dried beans soaked
 overnight or 300 g (10 oz) fresh
 beans, neatly chopped
3 potatoes, 3 carrots, 3 leeks,
 3 tomatoes, 1 stick celery,
 1 large onion, 6 zucchini
 (courgette), all neatly chopped
750 g (1½ lb) borage or other green
 leafy vegetable, neatly chopped
Salt
Black pepper
45 mL (3 tablespoons) olive oil
225 g (8 oz) small penne-like pasta
50 g (1¾ oz) freshly grated
 Parmesan cheese*

PESTO SAUCE

*2 cloves garlic
25 g (1 oz) pine nuts
20 basil leaves
Salt
Pepper
25 g (1 oz) Parmesan cheese
45 mL (3 tablespoons) olive oil*

THIS DELICIOUS SOUP from Liguria is a meal in itself. It is related to the French *pistou*. You can use whatever vegetables are available. Only attempt this soup when fresh basil is at hand. Don't try it with ready-made pesto sauce.

Method: Heat 1 L (1¾ pt) of lightly salted water and add all the vegetables. Season and pour in the olive oil. Traditionally the vegetables are cooked for about 2 hours but as soon as the beans are cooked I like to reduce the soup over a fierce heat if it is too watery to avoid overcooking the green vegetables.

To make the pesto sauce, process all the ingredients together.

Throw in the pasta and when it is cooked remove from the heat and stir in the pesto sauce. Check the seasoning and serve sprinkled with Parmesan cheese.

In Liguria they say the soup should be thick enough to hold a wooden spoon upright.

PUMPKIN AND WHITE BEANS

Zucca gialla e fagioli (in dialect: cucuzza e fasuoli)

*250 g (9 oz) fresh or dried white
   beans
Salt
45 mL (3 tablespoons) olive oil
2 cloves garlic, minced
500 g (1 lb) yellow pumpkin, finely
   sliced
2 bay leaves
Cayenne pepper
Fennel seeds*

I FIND THE COMBINATION of tastes very interesting in this recipe from Basilicata in the south.

Method: If you are using dried beans soak overnight in cold water. Drain and cook in boiling water until tender. Drain and season to taste.

Heat the oil, add the garlic and remove and discard once it has begun to change colour. Cook the pumpkin in the oil with the bay leaves, a little salt and cayenne pepper. Cover and cook very gently, adding a little water if necessary. When it is soft remove the bay leaves and purée the pumpkin. Stir in the cooked beans and a scattering of fennel seeds.

BROAD BEANS AND GREEN LEAFY VEGETABLE
Fave e cicoria

*200 g (7 oz) dried, skinned broad
     beans or 500 g (1 lb) fresh,
     shelled beans*
Salt
1 kg (2 lb) chicory or spinach
*Very good quality extra virgin olive
     oil*
Black pepper
*Optional — 1 carrot, 1 onion, 1
     stick celery, 1 potato, all roughly
     chopped*

THE ITALIAN cicoria (chicory), either wild or
cultivated, is a green leaf vegetable with a bitter
taste. If you cannot find an equivalent you can use
sorrel or spinach.

This dish is very good and really has to be tasted
before you can appreciate how well the flavours
combine. The recipe comes from Puglia where the
women used to work long hours in the fields with the
men. For this reason most of the traditional dishes
from that region can either be prepared at the last
minute, like many of the pasta sauces, or left alone to
cook slowly in the embers of the fire. The original
version of this dish used dried, skinned broad beans
which were soaked during the day then cooked
overnight in an earthenware pot in the fireplace. The
cicoria were cooked at the last minute and the
success of this simple dish lies in the quality of the
olive oil. It is not worth attempting with inferior oil.

I have made a lighter version using fresh broad
beans and spinach, which everyone loves, but you
have to pop the skins off the cooked fresh beans.

Method: Soak the dried beans for at least 12 hours
then cook in 1 L (1¾ pt) of lightly salted boiling water
on a very low heat for 3 hours. If you want to cook
the version with the extra vegetables add them for
the last 25 minutes.

Strain the beans and vegetables (if used) and purée
them. Pour the purée onto a plate and allow to dry
for about 30 minutes.

Cook the leafy vegetable quickly in boiling water
taking care not to overcook and spoil the colour.
Drain very well and serve each plate with the beans
on one side and the *cicoria* on the other side. Pour a
little oil on top and add black pepper to taste.

RADICCHIO WITH BEAN PURÉE

Radicchio con purea di fagioli

250 g (9 oz) white beans
1 stick celery, chopped
1 carrot, chopped
1 small onion, chopped
1 bay leaf
1 rasher streaky bacon, chopped
500 g (1 lb) radicchio
Salad dressing made from 50 mL
*   (3½ tablespoons) olive oil, 25*
*   mL (1¾ tablespoons) wine*
*   vinegar*
Black pepper
Salt
30 mL (2 tablespoons) extra virgin
*   olive oil*

AN INTERESTING, healthy antipasto using the unusual combination of radicchio and beans.

Method: Soak the beans for at least 12 hours then cook in boiling water with the celery, carrot, onion, bay leaf and bacon. When the beans are tender discard the other ingredients and purée the beans with about 350 mL (12 fl oz) cooking liquid to make a smooth cream.

Arrange the radicchio leaves on a plate and pour over the vinaigrette dressing. Season the bean purée and spoon over the salad, garnishing with a fine thread of olive oil.

BEAN SALAD IN ANCHOVY SAUCE

Fagioli in salsa di acciuga

350 g (12 oz) borlotti beans
Salt
Black pepper
20 mL (1½ tablespoons) olive oil
2 cloves garlic, minced
6 anchovy fillets, chopped
30 mL (2 tablespoons) wine
   vinegar
Parsley, chopped

I FIND THIS ANCHOVY dressing works a touch of magic with the prosaic beans.

Method: Soak the beans for at least 12 hours then cook in boiling water for about 25 minutes until tender. Drain well and season lightly because the anchovies are salty.

Heat the oil, add the garlic and let it begin to change colour before adding the anchovies which must be pushed with a wooden spoon so that they 'melt' into the oil. Pour on the vinegar and let it evaporate before stirring in the beans. Cook for a few minutes then turn into a serving dish. Garnish with parsley.

This dish is usually served cold.

CREAM OF SWEET YELLOW PEPPERS

Passato di peperoni gialli

*60 mL (4 tablespoons) extra virgin
   olive oil*
*1 medium sized onion, finely
   chopped*
1 carrot, finely chopped
1 stick celery, finely chopped
4 large Italian yellow peppers
4 medium sized potatoes, sliced
750 mL (1¼ pt) rich meat stock
2 bay leaves
200 mL (7 fl oz) milk
Salt
Pepper
*30 g (1 oz) Parmesan cheese,
   freshly grated*

THIS SUBTLE SOUP with its velvety texture and
delicate flavour makes a light, elegant summer
starter. I serve it in small white Japanese bowls to
enhance its vibrant colour.

Method: Heat the oil and cook the onion, carrot and
celery until the onion is golden brown. Remove the
seeds and tough fibres from the peppers and roughly
chop. Add these and the potatoes to the fried mixture
and add enough stock to cover the vegetables. Cover
the pan and cook slowly until the potatoes are soft.

Pass the mixture through a fine food mill to purée
and to remove the pepper skins which would spoil
the texture of the soup. Reheat gently, adding the bay
leaves and milk. Season to taste.

Serve hot with a little freshly grated Parmesan.
(Do not use ready-grated cheese.) Three or four
croutons can be scattered on top if desired.

AUBERGINE (EGGPLANT) CROQUETTES IN TOMATO SAUCE

Polpette di melanzana (in dialect: Purpette 'i milangiane)

500 g (1 lb) aubergine (eggplant)
2 slices stale bread with the crusts removed
3 cloves garlic
Parsley
50 g (1¾ oz) freshly grated pecorino or Parmesan cheese
Salt
Black pepper
Fresh breadcrumbs
Oil for deep frying
Tomato sauce (see Aubergine (Eggplant) Timbales with Tomato and Basil Sauce, page 49). If you want to make it more authentic small pieces of sweet green pepper may be cooked in the sauce.

CALABRIA HAS VERY interesting vegetable recipes which are part of the *cucina povera* tradition. I love them and they are ideal for people wanting to avoid meat and animal fats.

Method: Cook the aubergine in boiling salted water and drain well. In a food processor make a paste from the aubergine, stale bread, garlic, parsley and cheese. (In Calabria they use pecorino but I prefer the less strong flavour of Parmesan cheese.) Season the paste and leave in the refrigerator for an hour or more.

Roll the paste in your hands to form small sausage shapes. Coat with breadcrumbs and fry. If you prefer a crisper coating they can be dipped in beaten egg before the breadcrumbs.

Serve with some thick tomato sauce on the side of the plate.

SPINACH, MUSHROOM AND PARMESAN SALAD
Insalata di spinaci, funghi e parmigiano

600 g (1¼ lb) fresh young spinach
200 g (7 oz) button mushrooms
Salt
Black pepper
15 mL (1 tablespoon) extra virgin
  olive oil
50 g (1¾ oz) fresh Parmesan cheese
Lemon juice, to taste

ONE OF MY favourite light, easy starters and so healthy!

Method: Wash the spinach well, removing any stalks, and toss well to get rid of any water trapped in the crinkles. Using a wet sponge wash the mushrooms, dry, and finely slice. I usually use the thin blade in the food processor to get really thin slices.

Toss the whole spinach leaves with the mushrooms and season well, adding olive oil and using plenty of lemon juice to get a sharp tang.

Serve on individual plates or bowls, covered with very thin wafers of fresh Parmesan cheese.

FISH AND SHELLFISH

FISH

ITALY HAS A LONG coastline and Italians are never very far away from the sea. Over the centuries the Mediterranean, proudly called *mare nostrum* (our sea) by the Romans, has furnished the Italian kitchen with excellent, readily available *materia prima* (basic ingredients). Patrician Romans constructed stone fish-breeding tanks connected to the sea by intricate passageways to ensure a regular, fresh supply of fish. A preserved fish sauce, *garum,* was carried by the Roman legions as part of their 'iron rations'.

The Church rule that declared Friday a 'lean' day when no meat could be eaten has now been relaxed, but fish still figures prominently on Friday's menu at home and in restaurants.

Italians love fish, and today when the immediate sea yields a less rich catch, costly cargoes are flown in from North Africa and the Atlantic and Pacific oceans to maintain a colourful array of choice in the local markets.

The French believe that the success of a fish dish depends on the sauce in which it is served. This is the complete opposite of the Italian approach to cooking fish. Until recently fish was always served very simply with a touch of fresh herbs to bring out the good natural flavour. Any sauce was regarded with the suspicion that it could be disguising fish that was frozen or not very fresh. In many traditional restaurants, even today, platters of uncooked fish are brought to the table so that customers can inspect the eyes and gills for freshness; when the chosen fish has been grilled or roasted to order, it is presented in its entirety and only served off the bone on request.

The new style of Italian cooking tends to use fillets of fish which can be more quickly prepared to order. Here again herbs, vegetables, pulses, citrus fruits and virgin olive oil are used to enhance the flavour of the fish and heavy, creamy sauces are avoided.

Away from the Mediterranean it is sometimes difficult to find all the variety of fish and shellfish used in these recipes but do experiment with the choice available and substitute shelled prawns (shrimp) and frozen squid if that is all you can find. I would thoroughly recommend Alan Davidson's *Mediterranean Seafood* (Penguin Books, 1972) to help you search for the right fish.

FISH ZEPHYRS WITH SWEET PEPPER AND ZUCCHINI (COURGETTE) SAUCES

Involtini di sogliola

250 g (8 oz) fresh salmon
1 egg white
Salt
Black pepper
200 mL (7 fl oz) cream
6 fillets sole or other flat white fish

SWEET RED PEPPER SAUCE

2 large red peppers
Salt
Black pepper
A little good quality olive oil

ZUCCHINI (COURGETTE) SAUCE

300 g (10 oz) zucchini (courgette)
Salt
Black pepper
A little good quality olive oil

THIS IS AN ELEGANT dish that can be used as a starter or main course. The red, white and green — the colours of the Italian flag — give a patriotic flavour, and I often make this when the occasion calls for a homage to Italy!

Method: In a food processor pound the salmon to a smooth paste then add the egg white and season to taste. Gradually beat in the cream. Put this mousseline in the refrigerator for 30 minutes.

Lightly oil 6 small moulds and line the sides with the fish fillets, keeping the most attractive side outwards.

Fill the centre with the salmon mixture and smooth it over the top of the mould.

Cover with lightly greased paper and then with aluminium foil, pressing it in tightly over the rim of the mould. Cook for 20 minutes in a moderate oven, standing the moulds in a baking tin containing boiling water. After the moulds are cooked let them stand for 5 minutes before turning out.

Serve with red pepper and zucchini sauces.

To make the sweet red pepper sauce, roast the peppers and remove the skins, seeds and tough fibres. Purée to a smooth sauce, season to taste and add enough olive oil to make the sauce flow.

To make the zucchini sauce, lightly steam the zucchini so that they stay a good green. Purée to a smooth sauce, season to taste and add enough olive oil to make the sauce flow.

STEAMED PRAWNS (SHRIMP) IN CHICK PEA PUREE

Passatina di ceci con gamberi

100 g (3½ oz) dried chick peas
1 L (1¾ pt) salted water
1 clove garlic, peeled
2 sprigs rosemary
Salt
White pepper
12 large green prawns (shrimp),
shelled and central vein
removed
Extra virgin olive oil

TRADITIONALLY, ITALIAN cooking has many recipes that combine seafood and pulses. This is a 'new' recipe perfected by Fulvio Pierangelini for his restaurant Il Gambero Rosso at San Vincenzo in Tuscany. It is simple to prepare and can either be served on a flat plate as an antipasto, or, increasing the quantity of chick peas, in a soup bowl as a first course. It is essential to use good quality olive oil.

Method: Soak the chick peas for at least 10 hours. Cook them in the water with the garlic and rosemary. When they are soft make a thick purée using about half the cooking liquid. Season to taste.

Steam the prawns for a few minutes. Season to taste. Pour the chick pea purée into deep plates and arrange the prawns on top.

Just before serving, the dish is usually dressed with a fine swirl of excellent extra virgin olive oil.

FILLETS OF BRILL WITH ASPARAGUS AND ZABAIONE SAUCE

Rombo agli asparagi con zabaione

600 g (1¼ lb) green asparagus
6 fillets brill or other similar flat
white fish
Salt
Black pepper
1 bottle dry white wine, for
example Riesling
50 g (1¾ oz) butter
2 shallots, finely chopped
4 egg yolks
Fresh herbs, preferably basil,
parsley and chives, chopped

THIS IS A NEW dish which is comparatively easy but very effective. The zabaione must be made at the last minute.

Method: Clean the asparagus and cook lightly in a little boiling salted water so that they remain slightly underdone. Keep the cooking water, at least 400 mL (14 fl oz), for the sauce.

Place the fish fillets in a large shallow ovenproof dish so that they are not touching, and arrange the asparagus spears on top. Season with salt and pepper and dribble over a little of the wine. Dot with butter and cover the dish with aluminium foil so that it is completely sealed. Cook in a hot oven, 240°C (475°F), for just over 10 minutes. Keep the fish juices.

Put the shallots into a saucepan with 400 mL (14 fl oz) of the asparagus water, the fish juices and 400 mL (14 fl oz) white wine. Boil until you have only 200 mL (7 fl oz) liquid remaining then pour this liquid through a strainer.

Stand a pan in a larger pan of boiling water to make a bain-marie and whip in the egg yolks until you have a light, frothy zabaione sauce.

To serve place the fish on one side of the plate with the asparagus on the other side. Spoon over the zabaione sauce and sprinkle the fresh herbs and black pepper on top.

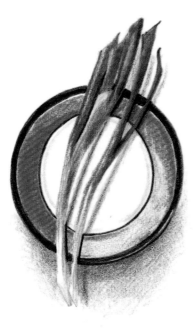

MUSSELS AND MARROW FLOWER SOUP

Zuppa di cozze e fiori di zucca

18 marrow flowers
1 kg (2 lb) mussels in their shells
2 cloves garlic, peeled and crushed
Parsley, chopped
1 small potato, finely sliced or 1
    tablespoon of corn meal mixed
    with a little water
15 mL (1 tablespoon) olive oil
1 small white onion, chopped
Salt
Pepper

THIS VERY UNUSUAL soup is a speciality of Livia and Alfonso Iaccarino who serve it in their restaurant, Don Alfonso, just outside Sorrento at Sant'Agata sui Due Golfi. I like to serve it in small white Japanese bowls or cups.

Method: Remove the stalk, stamens and pistils from the flowers and gently wash, pat dry, then chop roughly.

Scrub the mussels, discarding any broken or open shells, and remove the 'beard'.

Put the mussels in a saucepan with the garlic, parsley and about 750 mL (1¼ pt) water and heat over a high flame. As soon as the mussels have opened remove the pan from the heat and pour the liquid through a fine sieve. Thicken this liquid by adding the finely sliced potato or the corn meal and simmer for 15 minutes. Remove the mussels from their shells rejecting any that have failed to open.

Heat the oil in a frypan and fry the onion until it is soft. Add the marrow flowers and cook gently for about 5 minutes. Add the mussel liquid and purée. Season to taste.

Return the mixture to the saucepan and simmer for 10 minutes before adding the mussels.

This soup may be served hot or cold.

TUNA MOUSSE WITH GREEN BEANS

Mousse di tonno ai fagiolini

450 g (14½ oz) canned tuna
1 egg yolk
125 mL (4 fl oz) extra virgin olive
  oil
Salt
Pepper
50 mL (3½ tablespoons) cream,
  whipped
300 g (10 oz) fine, long green beans
Juice of 1 lemon

DURING THE LATTER HALF of the eighteenth century in Naples the great aristocratic families imported chefs from France and these *monsieurs* — soon to be dubbed *monzù* by the Neapolitans — started a great culinary tradition, still practised today, as they used their expertise to enhance the good local produce.

In the 1930s a comparatively modern *monzù*, Vincenzo Migliardi, created the following recipe when his 'family' found themselves with an unexpected royal guest, Umberto di Savoia, and a rather bare larder. Migliardi created a spectacular dish with the ingredients to hand and today it makes elegant dinner party fare.

Method: Drain the tuna and process it to a smooth paste.

Make a thick mayonnaise with the egg yolk and oil and blend in the fish. Season to taste.

Fold in the cream and spoon the mixture into a lightly oiled ring mould. Cover with aluminium foil and put in the freezer for several hours.

Quickly cook the beans in boiling salted water and when they are just tender plunge them into iced water to ensure they remain bright green. Toss in lemon juice when they are tepid.

Turn out the mould onto the serving plate and cover completely with the beans carefully arranged side by side. Put back into the refrigerator for 1 hour before serving.

I sometimes find the beans rather too thick, so after the mould has been in the freezer for 2 hours I slice the beans in half, lengthwise, and stick them to the frozen mousse with egg white. The mousse goes back into the refrigerator for 2 hours before serving.

WHITE FISH FILLETS WITH CEPS

Pesce con funghi porcini

15 g (½ oz) butter
1–2 fillets per person of any white
   fish
Salt
Black pepper
150 g (5 oz) ceps (mushrooms)
150 mL (5 fl oz) dry white wine
Juice of 1 lemon
Parsley, chopped
15 mL (1 tablespoon) olive oil

LIGURIAN RECIPES MAKE masterly use of wild mushrooms and fish. This simple recipe for 6 people combines both ingredients to make an unusually sumptuous main course.

Method: Butter an ovenproof dish and make a single layer of fish fillets. Add salt and a little freshly ground black pepper.

Wipe the mushrooms with a wet sponge to remove any earth or grit, dry carefully then arrange, thinly sliced, over the fish fillets. Season with salt and pepper.

Add the wine, being careful not to wash the seasoning off the mushrooms and cook in a pre-heated oven, 200°C (400°F), for 20 minutes.

Remove the fish with their mushroom topping to a warmed serving plate and process the cooking liquid with the lemon juice, parsley and olive oil. Spoon this sauce over the fish and serve at once.

TUNA MOUSSE IN POMEGRANATE JELLY

Spuma di tonno in gelatina di melograno

4 pomegranates
750 mL (1 ¼ pt) fish stock made
  from 1 stick celery, 1 carrot, 1
  small onion and any fish bits
  and pieces
Salt
Black pepper
6 gelatine sheets
400 g (14 oz) canned tuna in good
  olive oil, not brine

DON ALFONSO RESTAURANT outside Sorrento created this beautiful starter to use up some of the pomegranates weighing down their trees in early autumn. The delicate tuna mousse nestles in a bed of wine-coloured jelly. On my first introduction to this dish, as I greedily sucked the juicy pips decorating the plate, I began to sympathise with Persephone — maybe it was worth 6 months in Hades to enjoy such a treat!

Method: Using a juice extractor if available, extract the juice from 3 of the pomegranates and add it to the sieved fish stock. (For a good, delicate fish stock I usually plan to serve fillets of white fish for the main course and use the carcass and skin, boiled for 20 minutes with the vegetables. Failing this, a small whiting could be bought for the stock.) Season the pomegranate and stock mixture to taste, stir in the gelatine after softening it in a little water and place in the refrigerator for about 2 hours.

When the jelly begins to set, use a flat knife to smear a lining about 1 cm (½ in) thick all round the sides of a rectangular mould. Drain the oil from the tuna and purée. Season to taste and spoon into the space in the mould. Cover with the remaining jelly and leave to set in the refrigerator for about 2 hours. Then remove and keep in a cool place.

To serve, cut into slices and arrange on individual plates with a garnish of seeds from the remaining pomegranate.

SOUSED SMALL FISH

Sfogi in saor

1 kg (2 lb) small fish
Plain flour, for dusting
30 mL (2 tablespoons) olive oil
Salt
2 large onions, finely sliced
4 cloves
2 cm (¾ in) cinnamon stick
10 coriander seeds
250 mL (8 fl oz) wine
250 mL (8 fl oz) white wine
　vinegar
75 g (2½ oz) pine nuts
75 g (2½ oz) sultanas, soaked in a
　little warm water
Black pepper

THIS VENETIAN RECIPE dates from the fourteenth century when vinegar and spices were used to preserve food. The recipe can be used with sardines or any small fish. In Venice, traditionally, small soles are prepared in this way for the feast of the 'Redeemer' on the third Sunday in July. On the Saturday night a bridge of small boats stretches across to the island of Giudecca and amid fireworks, dancing, singing and drinking large quantities of *sfogi in saor* are readily consumed.

Method: Clean the fish, dry with kitchen paper and lightly dust with flour. Heat half the oil and fry the fish until they are golden brown on both sides. Put on kitchen paper to absorb any excess oil and lightly salt. Wipe out the pan, heat the remaining oil and gently fry the onions until they are soft and golden brown.

Grind the spices to a fine powder. Heat together the wine and vinegar. Stir in the ground spices and fried onions.

In a dish, terracotta if available, make a layer of small fish and cover with a little of the spiced liquid. Sprinkle on the nuts and drained sultanas, add a little pepper then make another layer of fish. Continue in this way until all the fish are covered with liquid.

Seal over with aluminium foil and leave to mature for 2 days in a cool place — not the refrigerator. Serve at room temperature.

DROWNED OCTOPUS
Polpi affogati

6 small polpi (octopuses)
6 cloves garlic
100 g (3½ oz) black olives, pitted
18 capers (optional)
600 g (1¼ lb) canned peeled
   Italian tomatoes, chopped
Parsley, chopped
30 mL (2 tablespoons) olive oil
Salt
Pepper

I FIRST DISCOVERED this Neapolitan speciality, while sitting on the wisteria-covered terrace of Posillipo's Rosiello restaurant. I fell in love with the restaurant and also the dish, which is usually cooked and served in small, individual earthenware pots. It is very easy to prepare. Make sure you choose small octopuses measuring about 8 cm (3¼ in) with a double row of suckers on the tentacles. The species with a single row of suckers are less expensive but they tend to be tough and rubbery. Incidentally, the local fishermen usually put a cork in the cooking liquid to ensure that the 'polpo' is tender. I get good results from this recipe even without the cork.

Method: Prepare 6 small pots with a cleaned, whole 'polpo' and the other ingredients. Season to taste, cover and cook slowly for 40 minutes in a pre-heated oven, 170°C (325°F).

CUTTLEFISH AND ARTICHOKE SOUP

Zuppa di seppie e carciofi

6 artichokes
Lemon
1 L (1¾ pt) vegetable stock made
    from carrot, onion, celery, 100
    mL (3½ fl oz) dry white wine
    and a bay leaf, plus the
    discarded artichoke leaves
3 cloves garlic, minced
30 mL (2 tablespoons) olive oil
6 medium sized cuttlefish, sliced
Parsley, chopped
Salt
Black pepper
300 g (10 oz) flour and 150 g (5 oz)
    butter or margarine for the
    pastry lids (optional), made in
    the usual way

LIGURIA MAKES GOOD use of an interesting combination of cuttlefish and artichokes. Various versions exist but my favourite entails serving the stew in individual ovenproof bowls which are topped with a crisp pastry lid. Just before the first delicious spoonful a smart tap to the crust sends crisp flakes into the rich, fragrant liquid.

By increasing the quantities this recipe can make a good main course.

Method: Clean the artichokes, removing the tough outer leaves and the stringy tops of the leaves. Cut the artichokes into 6 segments and remove the 'choke'. The cut artichokes must be rubbed with lemon and placed in a bowl of water and vinegar or lemon juice to prevent them changing colour.

Make a vegetable stock with the discarded artichoke leaves added to the stock vegetables.

Add the garlic to the heated oil and when it begins to change colour add the rinsed and dried artichokes, a few segments at a time. Let the artichokes change colour then add a little water, cover and stew for 10 minutes. Remove with a slotted spoon and keep aside.

Brown the cuttlefish in the same oil, remove and then simmer for about 30 minutes in the sieved vegetable stock with the parsley added. Leave the cuttlefish to cool in this cooking liquid for at least 2 hours. Season to taste and before serving re-heat and add the artichokes.

If you want to make pastry lids spoon the soup into ovenproof bowls and seal a pastry crust over the top. Brown in a hot oven for 10 to 15 minutes.

POZZUOLI FISH SOUP

60 mL (4 tablespoons) olive oil
4 cloves garlic, finely chopped
2 cuttlefish (seppie), cut into thin rings
200 mL (7 fl oz) dry white wine
500 g (1 lb) Italian tomatoes, peeled and chopped
2 tablespoons parsley, chopped
2 stone bass (lucerna), cleaned but with the head and skin left intact
3 small Mediterranean lobster
18 cm (7 in) moray eel (murena), cut into 3 cm (1 in) long pieces
2 tub fish (cuoccio)
3 small black rock scorfano (a red fish the French call rascasse, essential for Mediterranean soups)
10 prawns (shrimp), with the central vein removed by the head and its shell left intact
20 shellfish made up of mussels (cozze), razor shells (cannolicchio), wedge shells (telline), and carpet shells (vongola varace), washed under running water

POZZUOLI WAS THE most important Mediterranean port until Nero set up Ostia Antica just outside Rome. Today it has a thriving fish market and the local fish soup is a one-course feast.

This delicious version of the local speciality was prepared for me by Carlo Causa, fish chef at the Damiani family's Country Club Averno. Carlo shuns the traditional soup saucepan and cooks his soup over the flame in a large flat rectangular baking tin usually used for vast lasagne. In this way the fish is cooked in a single layer, with every fish coming into direct contact with the heat. It is important to add the ingredients in the order given opposite. If you cannot find the same fish use other varieties but try to balance the flavours.

Method: Heat the oil, add the garlic and let it begin to change colour before adding the cuttlefish. After a few minutes pour in the wine and when it begins to bubble add the tomatoes and parsley. Add the stone bass and after 5 minutes the lobster. The moray eel is added about 5 minutes after the lobster. Add the tub fish 10 minutes later.

This soup is not very liquid so the fish should be frequently turned to ensure even cooking. The scorfano can be put in almost immediately after the tub fish unless they are very small. Add the prawns to the soup 10 minutes after the last fish, then add the shellfish. Cook for 5 minutes more.

This soup must be served at once. It is very thick so it is usually presented on a deep serving plate together with thick rounds of toasted bread.

SEA BASS WITH LEMON AND MANDARIN SAUCE

Spigola al limone e mandarino

1 lemon
1 mandarin
1 sea bass, or similar fine fish,
*   weighing 1.5 kg (3 lb)*
Oregano
1 clove garlic
Salt
Black pepper
15 mL (1 tablespoon) extra virgin
*   olive oil*
100 mL (3½ fl oz) dry white wine
100 mL (3½ fl oz) lightly salted
*   water or fish stock*
Parsley, chopped

AS YOU SERVE THIS unusual, elegant fish course inspired by the incomparable Sicilian citrus fruits, the perfume will conjure up visions of a beautiful, lush island, shimmering in a heat haze that is only relieved by sporadic gusts of scent coming from the orange and lemon groves.

Method: Using a zester make fine threads of lemon and mandarin peel using ¾ of the fruit. Keep the remaining portion of the two peels and stuff inside the fish with the oregano and garlic. Season the fish, place in a lightly oiled baking tin then cook in a pre-heated oven, 200°C (400°F), for 5 minutes.

Squeeze half the lemon and both halves of the mandarin, and stir the juice into the wine. After the initial 5 minutes moisten the fish with this liquid and cook for another 5 minutes.

Now add the water (or fish stock) and cook for 25 minutes. Remove the fish to a heated plate and divide into fillets.

Mix together the filtered cooking liquid and the fruit juice and stir in the finely chopped parsley and threads of peel. Spoon the sauce over the fillets and serve at once.

RED MULLET WITH FENNEL SEEDS

Triglie al finocchio

6 mullet about 15 cm (6 in) long
100 g (3½ oz) streaky bacon,
*   roughly chopped*
Parsley, chopped
1 tablespoon fennel seeds, crushed
15 mL (1 tablespoon) olive oil
Salt
Black pepper

TRADITIONALLY, THIS SICILIAN recipe uses whole fish. The fish is cleaned but the head and skin are left intact. The fish is usually stuffed with the fennel paste and a few sprigs of wild fennel, or the feathery leaves from a fennel bulb. I prefer to use filleted mullet as this way the fish seems to absorb more flavour. If you prefer to use whole fish increase the cooking time to 20 minutes.

Method: Fillet the fish without removing the skin. In a food processor make a paste from the bacon, parsley and fennel seeds. Lightly oil a rectangular dish and lay the fillets in a single layer with the skin upwards. Sprinkle with salt and freshly ground black pepper then spread the paste evenly over the fillets. Cover with aluminium foil and bake in a pre-heated oven, 200°C (400°F), for 8 minutes.

HAKE BAKED IN A SEALED BAG

Nasello in cartoccio

12 small hake fillets
3 potatoes, finely sliced
150 g (5 oz) Italian tomatoes,
*   peeled*
18 black olives, pitted
Parsley, chopped
Salt
Black pepper
100 mL (3½ fl oz) dry white wine
30 mL (2 tablespoons) lemon juice
1 egg white

THIS LIGHT TASTY main course is easily prepared and can be made with any white fish fillets.

Method: Cut 6 large squares of baking paper or aluminium foil and lay 2 fish fillets on each. Cover with potato, tomatoes, olives, parsley, salt and freshly ground black pepper. Moisten with the wine and lemon juice, fold over to make a parcel sealing the edges with a little egg white. Pleat the aluminium foil or kitchen paper well to ensure that the edges are really sealed.

Cook for 25 minutes in a pre-heated oven, 200°C (400°F).

Serve in the paper so that the diners can open their own parcel and savour the aroma that escapes.

GOOD FRIDAY SOUP

Zuppa del venerdi santo

1 kg (2 lb) unshelled green prawns
  (shrimp) or lobster
2 L (3½ pt) fish stock made from
  the washed heads and shells, 1
  stick celery, 1 carrot, 1 small
  onion, bay leaf, salt and pepper
500 g (1 lb) peeled Italian tomatoes
45 mL (3 tablespoon) olive oil
2 whole salted anchovies or
  6 fillets, finely chopped
4 cloves garlic, finely chopped
Parsley, chopped
Cayenne pepper
Salt
Thick slices of bread to toast

GOOD FRIDAY IS not a public holiday in Italy and even twenty years ago I remember being really surprised to see people in restaurants tucking into their steaks and chicken. In the past, however, when Friday was still a 'lean' day for the Church, this soup was traditional Good Friday fare for the Romans. It is much simpler than most fish soups and I happily recommend it for any day of the year.

Method: Clean the shellfish and make the stock by boiling all the stock ingredients together for 20 minutes.

Purée the tomatoes and stir into the fish stock. Heat the oil and add the anchovies, garlic and parsley. When the garlic begins to change colour add the filtered stock and simmer for 20 minutes.

Cut the shellfish into thin strips and add to the soup. Cook for a further 5 minutes then add the cayenne pepper and check the salt.

Toast the bread and put at the bottom of the soup bowl before pouring on the hot soup. Serve before the toast has time to get too soggy.

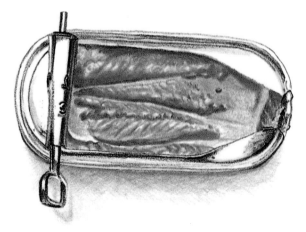

FISH AND GREEN BEANS IN BASIL SAUCE

Sogliola al Basilico

*6 soles, skinned and filleted,
    keeping the carcasses for the
    stock*
Juice of 3 lemons
200 mL (7 fl oz) dry white wine
Salt
Pepper
1 small onion, chopped
1 carrot, chopped
1 stick celery, chopped
30 mL (2 tablespoons) olive oil
300 g (10 oz) thin green beans
1 bunch fresh basil
50 g (1¾ oz) pine nuts

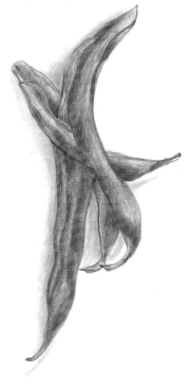

THE LIGHT GREEN sauce makes this an attractive dish and the perfume of the basil conjures up dreams of delectable meals eaten on sunlit terraces overlooking the Ligurian sea with a glass of chilled *Cinque Terre* wine close to hand.

Method: Marinate the sole fillets in 15 mL (1 tablespoon) of the lemon juice, 100 mL (3½ fl oz) of the white wine, salt and pepper.

Cook the chopped vegetables in half the olive oil then add 50 mL (3½ tablespoons) white wine, the fish carcasses and enough water to cover them. Bring to the boil then cook to make a concentrated stock. Pour through a sieve and put the liquid to one side.

Heat the remaining oil and lightly sauté the fish fillets for 3 minutes before adding the remaining white wine. Simmer for 2 or 3 minutes then remove the fillets and keep warm. Pour the marinade liquid and fish stock into the pan and bring to the boil. Remove from heat.

Cook the green beans in briskly boiling salted water until they are barely tender. Drain and season with lemon juice.

Process the basil leaves and pine nuts to make a smooth paste then gradually add the fish liquid.

Pour some of the sauce onto a large serving dish and arrange the sole fillets on top. The green beans should be piled around the edges of the plate. Add more sauce if necessary but take care not to drown the dish.

SMALL JEWEL BOXES OF PRAWNS (SHRIMP) AND ZUCCHINI (COURGETTE)

Scrigno di zucchini e gamberi

100 g (3½ oz) fresh breadcrumbs
30 g (1 oz) Parmesan cheese, grated
Parsley, mint and oregano, chopped
½ tablespoon cayenne pepper
Salt
24 large green prawns (shrimp), shelled and central vein removed
Olive oil
6 zucchini (courgette), finely sliced lengthwise

THIS IS A USEFUL dish for dinner parties because it can be prepared in advance and the size and quantity of prawns determines whether it is to be served as first or main course. It is served in individual oven-proof dishes.

Method: Mix together the breadcrumbs, cheese, herbs, pepper and salt. Dry the prawns. Lightly oil the dishes and line the bottom with half the slices of zucchini. Cover this layer with half the breadcrumb mixture and arrange the prawns on top. Lightly season the prawns then sprinkle half the remaining breadcrumb mixture on top. Dot with oil then cover with the remaining slices of zucchini. Make a final layer of breadcrumbs and dot with a few drops of oil.

Cover each dish with aluminium foil and just before serving cook in a pre-heated oven, 200°C (400°F), for 10 minutes.

MUSSELS BAKED IN THEIR SHELLS
Cozze gratinate

Fresh parsley, chopped
4 cloves garlic, chopped
1 tablespoon grated fresh ginger,
*   optional, not traditional*
40 g (1½ oz) fresh breadcrumbs
Salt
Black pepper
Grated peel 1 lemon
1 kg (2 lb) mussels in their shell
30 mL (2 tablespoons) olive oil
1 lemon cut into wedges

I REMEMBER VIVIDLY the first time I ate this dish. It was many years ago in a small trattoria in Trastevere — the 'other' side of Rome's river Tiber — where the people pride themselves on being 'real' Romans, and the waiters have never heard that 'the customer is always right'. This particular waiter listened to our dinner order but informed me that I would have the mussels instead of my choice of figs and prosciutto. He ignored my protests, stating firmly that I would love 'his' mussels. He was right of course and I find this version never fails to convert those who are a little wary about mussels.

My original waiter would probably be equally ruthless about my heretical suggestion of adding a little grated fresh ginger to the filling.

Method: Mix the parsley, garlic (and ginger) with the breadcrumbs, salt and pepper, and lemon peel.

Scrub the mussels, removing the 'beard' and any encrustments and put them with a little water into a large pan. Cover and heat fiercely so that the shells open. Discard any mussels that have failed to open.

Put 2 mussels into 1 half-shell and sprinkle with the breadcrumb mixture. Add a few drops of oil and place the shells on a baking tray in a hot oven for a few minutes until they are golden brown.

Serve with wedges of lemon so that each person can squeeze on the amount of juice they prefer.

CUTTLEFISH AND POTATOES IN HELL

Seppie all' inferno con patate

100 mL (3½ fl oz) olive oil
4 cloves garlic, chopped
Parsley, chopped
1 hot chilli pepper, chopped with
    seeds removed to avoid it being
    too hot
1 kg (2 lb) cuttlefish, cleaned and
    cut into strips
200 mL (7 fl oz) dry white wine
750 g (1½ lb) potatoes
Salt

I LEARNED THIS old Ligurian speciality from Giuseppe Menconi, a notable gourmet who has rescued from oblivion many simple traditional dishes.

In the past the women placed their heavy flat irons on the casserole lid to ensure that none of the flavour escaped with the steam. Choose a pan with a well-fitting lid so that you gain the same effect. The touch of 'hell' comes from the hot chilli.

Method: Heat the oil in a heavy pan and add the garlic, parsley and chilli pepper. When the garlic begins to change colour add the cuttlefish and cover with the white wine. Season to taste. Simmer very slowly for 30 minutes then check to make sure that the fish is tender.

Now add the potatoes cut into wedges and a little hot stock if necessary, but be careful not to make it too liquid. You need a thick stew not a soup. Before serving check seasoning.

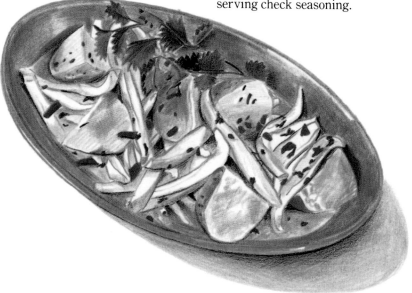

BREAM BAKED IN BREAD DOUGH WITH SCAMPI SAUCE

Dentice in crosta di pane con salsa di scampi

*1 large bream or similar fish,
    drained and cleaned, weighing
    about 1.5 kg (3 lb)*
2 cloves garlic, chopped
*Fresh mint, oregano, rosemary,
    basil, chopped*
15 mL (1 tablespoon) olive oil
Salt
Black pepper
*1 kg (2 lb) bread dough using your
    favourite bread recipe*
5 g (¹/₅ oz) butter

SAUCE

250 g (9 oz) unshelled scampi
200 mL (7 fl oz) dry white wine
*Fresh mint, oregano, rosemary,
    basil, chopped*
1 large bunch basil
30 mL (2 tablespoons) olive oil
Salt
Black pepper

THIS INTERESTING DISH comes from Nino Statella's Catanian restaurant, Poggio Ducale. Although it is not a traditional Sicilian recipe the combination of Mediterranean aromas used with good *materia prima* gives it a tang of the south.

Method: Clean the fish and stuff the inside with the garlic and fresh herbs. Brush with oil, season and wrap in the bread dough which should be rolled out not too thinly. Seal the edges well and put in a buttered ovenproof dish. Cook at 200°C (400°F), for 40 minutes.

To make the sauce, shell the scampi and boil the scampi heads and shells in the wine with an equal amount of water, and the fresh herbs. Let this stock reduce a little then pour through a strainer. Add the scampi and cook for a further 5 minutes.

Process the basil leaves and oil then stir into the sauce. Season to taste.

Serve the fish in bread dough in slices with a spoonful of the scampi sauce at the side.

POULTRY

POULTRY

IN ANCIENT ROME geese were raised not necessarily for the table but to act as watch-dogs. Rome's Capitoline Hill was saved from treacherous attack when the Temple of Juno's geese sounded the alarm. (My neighbours' geese bear witness to their effectiveness as watch-dogs, with non-stop, maniacal cackles unfailingly marking my comings and goings.) The Romans fattened up other geese to eat and overfed them in order to enlarge their livers, thus starting the *foie gras* tradition. They also loved to eat doves, ducks, turkeys and peacocks, although the poet, Horace, found little difference between the taste of peacock and chicken.

The consumption of chicken was periodically controlled by laws to safeguard the egg supply and reinforce various religious practices. Only a limited number of chickens could be fattened up for cooking, and only one specially fed chicken could be served at a time. The ordinary chickens were rather stringy and scrawny so they were regarded as common fare. Today the fear of hormone-laced feed has reversed the value of free range poultry and the thinner *pollo ruspante* — the chicken that scratches the ground to find its food — is more expensive and more sought after.

Traditionally, every family used to keep its own poultry and even nowadays in the country and the outskirts of large cities the *cortile,* or courtyard animals, are reared for the table. This probably explains why poultry is regarded as fare for every day rather than high days and holidays. In Rome there are several small poultry farms breeding and selling free range birds. I am afraid I am too squeamish to choose my live victim and hear it squawking on its way to have its neck wrung. By ordering from the local butcher I manage to distance myself from the process!

DUCK IN RED WINE VINEGAR

Anitra in aceto di vino rosso

30 mL (2 tablespoons) olive oil
4 cloves garlic, whole and peeled
3 large onions, divided into 8
    segments
2 sprigs rosemary
2 ducks each weighing about 1.2 kg
    (2½ lb)
Salt
5 cloves
3 cm (1 in) stick cinnamon,
    ground to a coarse powder
1 L (1¾ pt) red wine vinegar
1 L (1¾ pt) meat stock

THIS IS A RECIPE from Piedmont and usually the cleaned duck is covered with boiling, lightly salted water and cooked for 15 minutes to eliminate the excessive fat. This method, used for most poultry, is known as *dare l' acqua*.

Method: Heat the oil and add the garlic, the onions and the rosemary. When the garlic begins to change colour remove and reserve the onions and garlic and brown the ducks on all sides. (If you have used the boiling water technique described above drain the ducks on paper towels before putting into the hot oil.)

Now rub the duck with the salt, sprinkle the cloves and cinnamon around and put the duck, onions and garlic into a roasting pan, pouring off any excess fat. Cook for 30 minutes at 150°C (300°F).

After 30 minutes pour over the wine vinegar and continue to cook very slowly for 45 minutes. Now add the stock and cook for a further 45 minutes.

At the end of this time the vinegar and stock will have reduced to form a rich aromatic sauce which should be served as a dressing for the thick slices of duck.

CHICKEN BREAST WITH HAZELNUTS

Petti di pollo alle nocciole

100 g (3½ oz) shelled hazelnuts,
*   coarsely ground*
6 tablespoons fresh breadcrumbs
600 g (1¼ lb) chicken breast cut
*   into fillets*
Salt
Black pepper
60 g (2 oz) butter
6 sage leaves

HAZELNUTS HAVE ALWAYS played an important role in Piedmontese cooking and this recipe uses a traditional ingredient in a new way.

Method: Mix the hazelnuts with the breadcrumbs.

Season the chicken with salt and pepper and warm for a few minutes over a low heat in the melted butter and sage leaves. Do not let the chicken brown. Remove the chicken fillets and coat them with the hazelnut mixture.

Arrange in a single layer in an ovenproof dish and cook for 10 minutes at 150°C (300°F). If the fillets are thick they may need longer cooking time.

I like to serve this with a sauce made from 90 mL (6 tablespoons) extra virgin olive oil, 45 mL (3 tablespoons) lemon juice, salt and black pepper.

TEPID CHICKEN SALAD WITH ARTICHOKE HEARTS AND BLACK OLIVES

Insalata tiepida di pollo, carciofi e olive

*1 chicken, boned and cut in half
    (try to keep 2 long lengths of
    skin)*
*A mixture of fresh herbs including
    tarragon, chives, thyme, sage
    and rosemary, chopped*
Salt
Black pepper
15 mL (1 tablespoon) olive oil
*60 mL (4 tablespoons) dry white
    wine*
6 artichoke hearts
½ lemon
1 tablespoon chopped mint
Radicchio and green salad leaves
18 small black olives, pitted
*Salad dressing made with 100 mL
    (3½ fl oz) extra virgin olive oil,
    50 mL (3½ tablespoons) lemon
    juice, salt and black pepper*

THIS IS AN ADAPTATION from one of the rabbit dishes served in Alessandro Franceschetti's Florence restaurant, La Vecchia Cucina. It makes an unusual starter or a light main course for a summer dinner party.

Method: Flatten out one chicken half and cover with half the herbs, salt and pepper. Roll carefully (it does not matter if you have 2 pieces) to form an oblong parcel and wrap 1 piece of skin round the outside. It must form small rounds when sliced. If the skin is in pieces, overlap them slightly. Season, brush with olive oil and roll tightly in aluminium foil. Repeat the process with the other half.

Cook in the oven at 220°C (425°F), for 20 minutes then open the foil and cook for another 10 minutes. Sprinkle with wine, enclose in fresh foil and allow to cool.

The artichokes should be cooked in boiling, salted water with half a lemon. Divide the hearts into quarters and sprinkle with the mint and a little warm olive oil.

Arrange the salad leaves on a large serving platter and make an overlapping row of thin chicken slices down the middle. The texture is best when the chicken is tepid. It can also be served at room temperature. Scatter the artichokes and olives over the plate and add a little dressing. The rest of the dressing can be served separately in a small jug.

GUINEAFOWL WITH ORANGE AND GRAPE SAUCE

Faraona con uva e arance

2 guineafowl
1 onion, roughly chopped
1 carrot, roughly chopped
1 stick celery, roughly chopped
Salt
75 g (2½ oz) lard
3 shallots, finely chopped
150 g (5 oz) sultanas soaked in a
*   little wine*
Black pepper
400 mL (14 fl oz) dry white wine
6 oranges
1 small bunch of black grapes
1 small bunch of white grapes

I LOVE TO COOK this for dinner parties because it can be prepared well in advance. If it is cooked and allowed to cool the bird seems to absorb more of the flavour. The grapes, however, must not be added until a few minutes before serving.

Method: Clean the guineafowl and place in a large pan covered with boiling water, together with the onion, carrot and celery. Add a little salt, cover and cook for 15 minutes.

Remove from the pan and cut into quarters.

Melt the lard in another pan and add the shallots and the drained sultanas. Cook over a low heat for 5 minutes then add the guineafowl portions and turn up the heat so that they brown. Season to taste, then add the wine and the juice of 4 of the oranges. Cover and cook slowly for another 30 minutes.

Peel the remaining oranges and cut into thin slices.

Halve the grapes and remove the seeds. The grapes should be stirred into the guineafowl mixture about 3 minutes before removing from the heat. Arrange the bird on a heated serving plate surrounded by sauce and decorated with the orange slices.

CHICKEN ROMAN STYLE

Pollo alla Romana

2 red sweet peppers
2 green sweet peppers
45 mL (3 tablespoons) olive oil
4 cloves garlic, finely chopped
12 small chicken portions (2 per
    person) or 2 young chickens,
    each cut into 6 pieces
Salt
Black pepper
200 mL (7 fl oz) dry white wine
400 g (14 oz) canned Italian plum
    tomatoes, chopped

MOST ROMAN TRATTORIAS offer this on their daily menu. It is traditionally made with a not too plump bird so that the enticing flavour of the sweet peppers penetrates down to the bone which in turn imparts its own flavour. So, I suggest for this recipe you do not use only boneless chicken breasts.

Method: Remove the seeds and tough fibres from the sweet peppers and cut into segments about 3 cm (1¼ in) wide.

Heat the oil, add the garlic and when it begins to change colour put in the washed and dried chicken pieces. Brown them on all sides then season to taste. Pour on the wine and simmer on a low flame for 5 minutes. Now add the tomatoes and the sweet peppers. Cook slowly in a covered pan for 45 minutes. Check the seasoning and serve.

This dish can be prepared ahead of time as it reheats quite well.

CHICKEN WITH BLACK OLIVES

Pollo con le olive

3 onions
30 g (2 tablespoons) fennel seeds
Salt
Black pepper
2 sprigs rosemary 12 cm (5 in)
* long or 30 g (2 tablespoons)*
* dried rosemary*
6 bay leaves
1 roasting chicken weighing about
* 1.5 kg (3 lb)*
30 mL (2 tablespoons) olive oil
3 cloves garlic, chopped
250 mL (8 fl oz) dry white wine
150 g (5 oz) black olives

AN EASY RECIPE from Tuscany using fennel seeds and black olives to transform any old chicken into a succulent feast.

Method: Finely chop 1 onion and mix with half the fennel seeds and the salt, pepper, rosemary and 1 crumbled bay leaf. Rub the inside of the chicken with this mixture. Brush the skin with a little olive oil and sprinkle over the remaining fennel seeds and more salt and pepper.

Place the chicken in an oiled roasting dish, surrounded by remaining onions chopped, garlic and bay leaves.

Roast for just under 1 hour at 180°C (350°F). Sprinkle with white wine every 15 minutes.

After the hour baste the chicken, add the olives and cook for another 10 minutes.

Allow to stand in a warm place for 15 minutes before cutting into 6 portions with kitchen shears.

LEMON CHICKEN

Pollo al limone

2 lemons
30 mL (2 tablespoons) olive oil
1 stick celery, very finely chopped
1 carrot, very finely chopped
2 cloves garlic, very finely chopped
1 sage leaf
1 sprig thyme
1 sprig rosemary
6 black peppercorns, crushed
4 juniper berries, crushed
1 chicken cut into 6 fair sized
    joints, or 6 chicken portions
Flour for dusting
Salt
500 mL (16 fl oz) white wine
Chopped parsley

THIS SIMPLE CHICKEN dish is even more delicious if you manage to find the lovely dimpled Amalfi lemons.

Method: Using a zester make fine threads of lemon peel then squeeze the lemons.

Heat the oil and fry the vegetables, the herbs (not the parsley) and the crushed spices. Cook gently for 10 minutes then add the chicken pieces which have been lightly dusted with flour and salt. Brown quickly, then pour over the wine and lemon juice. Stir in half the lemon threads.

When the liquid comes to the boil transfer the chicken and the liquid to a baking dish and cook for about 45 minutes in an oven at 180°C (350°F).

Serve with the vegetable and herb liquid as a sauce, garnished with the chopped parsley and remaining lemon threads.

CHICKEN SALAD WITH BALSAMIC VINEGAR

Insalata di cappone al aceto balsamico

600 g (1¼ lb) capon breast, or plump chicken breast if not available
1 carrot, roughly chopped
1 stick celery, roughly chopped
1 small onion, roughly chopped
Salt
Pepper
1 lemon
50 mL (3½ tablespoons) sweet white wine
30 mL (2 tablespoons) extra virgin olive oil
30 mL (2 tablespoons) traditional balsamic vinegar
75 g (2½ oz) sultanas soaked in a little hot water

IN THE PAST, Mantova flourished under the benign autocracy of the Gonzaga family who were great patrons of art and music. The culinary arts were not neglected and the court chef, Bartolomeo Stefani, in 1622, published his collection of recipes. Mantova has retained this tradition of fine cooking and many Gonzagaan recipes can be enjoyed at Gaetano Martini's restaurant, Il Cigno.

Method: Cover the breast with a little boiling water, the vegetables and salt and pepper. Cook gently until tender. Discard the vegetables and stock and allow the chicken to cool.

Using a zester make fine threads of lemon peel.

Mix together the wine, olive oil and vinegar until they emulsify. Add the drained sultanas and lemon peel. Season to taste.

Slice the chicken evenly and pour on the sauce. Leave for 2 to 3 hours for the flavours to amalgamate before serving at room temperature, on a plate dressed with a little radicchio and thin strips of carrot.

ROAST TURKEY WITH POMEGRANATE
Paeta rosta al malgarano

1 small onion, chopped
1 young female turkey, weighing
  about 2 kg (4 lb)
Salt
1 orange (optional)
6 sage leaves
Black pepper
30 mL (2 tablespoons) olive oil
3 pomegranates

SAUCE

30 g (1 oz) butter
1 small onion, finely chopped
Turkey giblets, minced (optional)
300 mL (10 fl oz) stock, hot
Cooking juices from the turkey
Juice of 1 pomegranate

THE VENETO REGION gives us this lovely turkey recipe which normally uses a small female bird. I love the exotic effect of the pomegranate seeds and the purple sauce. The turkey can also be roasted on a spit but a pan must be placed below to collect the juices that are brushed frequently over the bird. The pomegranate juice is added after the first 1½ hours.

These quantities serve more than the usual 6 portions but the turkey can be served cold in a salad with an extra pomegranate the following day.

Method: Place the onion inside the cleaned turkey with a little salt. I usually include an unpeeled orange washed very well and pierced all over with a trussing needle. Add 2 or 3 sage leaves then sew up the bird. Rub a little salt, pepper and oil over the breast and place in a roasting tin with the remaining oil and sage leaves. Cook in a pre-heated oven, 190°C (375°F), for 1½ hours, turning the turkey frequently. Cover with a sheet of aluminium foil if it seems to be browning too quickly.

After the initial 1½ hour cooking period remove the turkey from the oven and brush all over with the juice from 2 of the pomegranates. (It is quite easy with a juice extractor to get the pomegranate juice without the pips but it is a little tiresome to do by hand with a sieve.)

Lower the oven temperature to 150°C (300°F) and return the turkey for another 1½ hours, basting frequently during this period.

Meanwhile remove the pips from the third pomegranate and keep to one side. Prepare the sauce.

To make the sauce, melt the butter and fry the onion
until soft. Add the minced giblets if you like to use
these, and cook for 5 minutes. Stir in the hot stock
and when the turkey is ready add the strained
cooking juices and the juice from the fourth
pomegranate.

Cut the turkey into large pieces (do not carve),
sprinkle with a little sauce and scatter the
pomegranate seeds on top. Put back in the hot oven
for 10 minutes. The rest of the sauce is served
separately.

MEAT

MEAT

MEAT HAS NEVER played a dominant role in Italian cooking. Oxen were raised to work on the land, not to be butchered, and in Roman times it was a capital offence to slaughter these valuable animals. Sheep and goats were kept since they needed less pasture land than cattle, but once they had outlived their usefulness in giving milk, their meat proved tough and rather tasteless. The wealthy preferred to eat very young lamb and kid and this preference is still seen today when young suckling lamb *(abbacchio)*, that has never tasted grass is the meat for special occasions. The sparse grazing land encourages the butchering of young animals and veal is more common than beef. The only region with a tradition of good beef is Tuscany where the *chianina* (cattle), bred by the Romans and Etruscans as fitting sacrifices to the pagan gods, were enjoyed by Renaissance princes at their great banquets.

Most households kept a pig, feeding it with kitchen scraps and whatever else came to hand. This versatile animal appeared on the table in many different ways and this is still true in Italian cooking. The people of Parma, renowned for their love of music and their veneration of the locally-born composer, Verdi, have a proverb: *I maiale è come la musica di Verdi, non c'è nulla da buttare via.* (The pig is like Verdi's music: nothing can be thrown away.)

Since meat was expensive, traditional recipes usually combine it with cheaper ingredients in order to make the meat go further. Larger cuts are usually cooked slowly with wine to improve the texture and flavour of the meat. There is not a tradition in the art of butchery, and even today most butchers do not prepare and cut meat in advance because this is not acceptable to the customer. If minced meat is required the meat is chosen first then minced and even steaks and chops are cut to order. Large roasting cuts do not exist and housewives insist that all visible fat is removed from their chosen thin slices. They cannot believe their eyes when they see me buying a 2 kg (4 lb) piece of beef to roast, liberally trimmed with fat. My butcher, Pino, declares that it takes an Englishwoman to understand meat! That might be true when it comes to roast beef, but the following recipes show how Italians use ingenuity to make delicious dishes from meat that is not always tender or naturally full of flavour.

VEAL ESCALOPE WITH BALSAMIC VINEGAR
Piccata all' aceto balsamico

6 thin slices of veal, beaten flat
Flour
Salt
Black pepper
30 mL (2 tablespoons) olive oil
30 g (1 oz) butter
100 mL (3½ fl oz) dry white wine
6 teaspoons balsamic vinegar

TRADITIONAL BALSAMIC VINEGAR is extremely costly because it cannot be mass produced. Only a handful of families living around Modena and Reggio Emilia have the skill and understanding to follow the complicated technique by which the vinegar is aged in a series of casks made of 5 different woods which in turn give a particular flavour to the vinegar. Some of the casks used date back to the sixteenth century and even the fumes are heady. Lucrezia Borgia, when married to the Duke of Modena, inhaled balsamic vinegar to alleviate the pangs of childbirth.

The balsamic vinegar produced commercially is only a very pale imitation and will not really do very much for the veal in this recipe but a few teaspoonfuls of the real stuff work sheer magic.

Method: Lightly flour and season the slices of veal and brown in the heated olive oil. Add the butter and when it has melted and coated the meat dribble on the wine. Just before serving add the balsamic vinegar.

SLIVERS OF VEAL OR BEEF WITH ROCKET

Stracetti alla rughetta

1 large bunch rocket
30 mL (2 tablespoons) olive oil
500 g (1 lb) wafer thin slices of
*   veal or beef, cut into thin slivers*
Salt
Black pepper

STRACETTI means little rags and this easy 'new' recipe uses thin slices similar to those served raw in *carpaccio*. It takes all of 5 minutes to prepare and the tangy *rughetta* (rocket) makes it one of my firm favourites.

Method: Wash and dry the rocket. Heat the oil in a large frying pan and stir in the slivers of meat. Season to taste and after stirring for 2 minutes add the rocket leaves. Cover and cook over a low heat for another 2 minutes.

A few extra drops of olive oil can be added before serving if desired.

STEWED VEAL WITH LENTIL SAUCE

Bocconcini di vitello alla crema di lenticchie

LENTIL SAUCE

250 g (9 oz) continental lentils,
*   preferably castelluccio*
1 stick celery, chopped
1 carrot, chopped
15 mL (1 tablespoon) olive oil
1 medium sized onion, finely
*   chopped*
200 g (7 oz) canned Italian
*   tomatoes, chopped*
Salt
Pepper

STEWED VEAL

30 mL (2 tablespoons) olive oil
3 cloves garlic, minced
6 sage leaves
Sprig rosemary
600 g (1¼ lb) lean veal, cut into
*   oblongs*
Salt
Pepper
100 mL (3½ fl oz) dry white wine
3 canned Italian tomatoes, chopped

THIS INTERESTING COMBINATION of veal and lentils was invented by the Umbrian chef, Angelo Paracucchi, for his restaurant in Ameglia.

For vegetarians, the lentil sauce can be made more liquid and served as a soup.

To make lentil sauce, soak the lentils overnight in cold water.

Drain and bring to the boil with the celery and carrot in a little lightly salted water.

Heat the oil and fry the onion until it becomes transparent then add the tomato and simmer for about 5 minutes. Add this to the lentils and cook for 20 minutes or until the lentils are soft. If necessary add a little water but the sauce needs to be thick. Check for seasoning, then purée the mixture.

To make the stewed veal, heat the oil and add the garlic, sage and rosemary. Add the seasoned meat and brown very quickly over a fierce flame. Pour over the wine and simmer until the meat is tender. Add the tomatoes and cook uncovered to reduce the sauce since it should provide a thick coating to the pieces of veal.

Pour the lentil sauce over each plate and serve the meat on top.

BEEF BRAISED IN BAROLO WINE

Brasato al barolo

Plain flour
A piece of good quality, lean beef,
*   weighing about 1 kg (2 lb)*
Salt
Black pepper
75 g (2½ oz) butter
1 bottle Barolo wine
1 onion, roughly chopped
1 stick celery, roughly chopped
2 carrots, roughly chopped
Fresh herbs — thyme, sage,
*   rosemary, parsley and bay leaf,*
*   all roughly chopped*

THICK SLICES OF beef served with its own rich sauce provide a sumptuous meal for a winter's day in Piedmont, the region that is the home of the great red wines.

Method: Lightly flour the meat and rub in a little salt and pepper. Melt the butter and when it is hot quickly sear all the surfaces of the beef. Pour over the wine and add the vegetables and herbs. Cover and cook for two hours in a moderate oven, 180°C (350°F).

Remove the meat, bay leaf and any herb stalks then purée the vegetables and gravy to make a thick sauce. Check the seasoning. Cut the meat into thick slices and spoon over a little sauce.

MEATBALLS WITH SAGE AND MARSALA WINE

Polpettine alla salvia

750 g (1½ lb) lean minced beef
12 sage leaves
90 g (3 oz) butter
40 g (1½ oz) Parmesan cheese
Salt
Pepper
100 mL (3½ fl oz) dry Marsala
   wine (or medium dry sherry if
   Marsala not available)

THERE ARE MANY different regional versions of meat-balls but they are more common in the south, where ingenuity was used to make a little meat go a long way. This one, and the following two are three of my favourite versions.

Here, the Sicilian Marsala wine is used to great effect.

Method: Mix the meat with the sage leaves, half the butter and the Parmesan cheese. Season to taste then leave the mixture to rest in the refrigerator for 30 minutes.

Form the paste into small balls a little larger than a walnut and brown them in the remaining butter. When they are cooked pour over the wine, let it evaporate for a few minutes then serve the meatballs in their own savoury gravy.

LEMON-FLAVOURED MEATBALLS

Polpettine

500 g (1 lb) lean veal
50 g (1¾ oz) fresh breadcrumbs
   from fine white bread
50 g (1¾ oz) freshly grated
   Parmesan cheese
30 g (1 oz) pine nuts
Grated peel of 2 medium lemons
15 mL (1 tablespoon) lemon juice
1 egg
Parsley, chopped
Salt
Black pepper
Oil for frying

THESE LIGHT MEATBALLS come from the island of Ischia and the dimpled Amalfi lemons add their own touch of magic. If you are in Ischia in the warm months it is worth the small taxi boat ride from Sant'Angelo to the restaurant Girasole to sample their *polpettine* after swimming in a sea pulsing with exciting thermal springs.

Method: In a food processor mix together all the ingredients to make a fine paste. If the mixture seems too dry add a little more lemon juice. Allow to rest for at least 30 minutes in the refrigerator before rolling into small balls about 4 cm (1½ in) in diameter. Flatten slightly with your thumb then fry them in the hot oil until golden brown on both sides.

   These meatballs are usually served with a *little* fresh tomato sauce, see page 49. If you use the tomato sauce it should only be a spoonful for each *polpettine* or you will drown the delicate flavour.

MEATBALLS WITH JULIENNE VEGETABLES

Polpette di Oretta

1 egg, beaten
50 g (1¾ oz) freshly grated
  Parmesan cheese
Parsley, chopped
Salt
Pepper
Nutmeg
500 g (1 lb) lean minced veal
1 slice white bread soaked in a
  little milk
15 mL (1 tablespoon) olive oil
30 g (1 oz) butter
150 g (5 oz) thin carrot strips
150 g (5 oz) onion, finely chopped
100 g (3½ oz) celery, finely chopped
Light chicken or vegetable stock, as
  needed
Juice of 2 lemons

ORETTA MODUGNO LIVES in Rome but her cooking reveals the deeply felt influence of her Tuscan and Neapolitan relatives. Oretta soaks the onion for about 12 hours in cold water, changing the water at least once to make the dish more delicate and digestible. I confess that I go right ahead with a freshly peeled onion. These meatballs have her own personal touch and I find them irresistibly different.

Method: Mix the egg, Parmesan, parsley, salt, pepper and nutmeg together with the minced veal. Add the moistened bread to the mixture after squeezing out the excess milk. Roll into little balls and put in a cool place to rest.

Heat the oil and butter and stir in the prepared vegetables. Add a little stock from time to time to prevent them browning. When the vegetables are soft add the meatballs and cook gently until they are golden brown. Add the lemon juice, simmer for a few minutes then serve.

BEEF COOKED IN RED WINE IN THE GRAND DUKE STYLE

Stracotto del Granduca

1 kg (2 lb) lean beef
Slivers of garlic, rosemary, pine
   nuts, toasted almonds and
   sultanas to be put into the meat
15 mL (1 tablespoon) olive oil
Salt
Pepper
1 stick celery, roughly chopped
6 carrots, roughly chopped
1 sprig rosemary
1 tablespoon sultanas
1 tablespoon pine nuts
1 tablespoon almonds
1 bottle red Tuscan wine

DURING THE RENAISSANCE fruit, nuts and spices were used with meat to add a note of opulence and to disguise the meat's lack of freshness. This *dolceforte* effect is not always to modern tastes but Dino, for his Florentine restaurant, has adapted a recipe which dates back to 1600 to produce a rich, pleasing dish.

Method: Tie the beef into an oblong with a diameter of about 12 cm (5 in). With a sharp, pointed knife make a series of deep incisions to be filled with the herbs, nuts and sultanas. Rub the meat with oil and season to taste.

Put the meat in an ovenproof dish surrounded by the vegetables, rosemary, sultanas and nuts. Cover loosely with aluminium foil and cook very slowly, 130°C (250°F), for about 2½ hours. Now remove the foil and add the wine. Cook for another 30 minutes.

The sauce should be processed to make a coarse purée and spooned over thick slices of beef.

SELECTED BOILED MEATS

Bollito misto

2 medium onions
4 leeks
500 g (1 lb) carrots
6 small turnips
1 head celery
Salt
Black pepper
1 piece of shin beef weighing about
  1 kg (2 lb)
1 boiling chicken or a piece of
  stewing veal
1 ham joint

PIEDMONT, LOMBARDY AND Emilia Romagna all lay claim to this sumptuous feast. Various meats are boiled together then served in thick slices with vegetables and spicy sauces like the *salsa verde* — a green sauce from Piedmont given in this recipe. It is also accompanied by a deliciously unusual preserve of whole fruit in a mustard-flavoured syrup. This *mostarda di frutta* is a speciality of Lombardy from Cremona and it can be made at home when the fruit is in season or bought in jars from Italian grocery shops.

Bollito misto can be seen in all its glory at Fini's restaurant in Modena. A great steaming trolley is wheeled to each table for the waiter to carve each customer's selection from beef, veal, ham, pork, tongue, capon and the huge sausage-like *zampone* or *cotechino.*

Although it is not worth preparing this dish for less than 6 people because of the quantities involved it can be made very successfully with only three different meats and the left-overs are equally good the next day. I usually use beef, chicken and ham.

Method: Clean the vegetables and chop into large pieces. Place in a large pan with 2 L (3½ pt) cold water, salt and pepper. When the water is boiling briskly, add the beef, making sure it is covered by the water. One hour later the veal or chicken is put in the pan and more boiling water added if necessary. The ham is usually cooked apart to avoid making the dish too salty. If you are using *zampone* or *cotechino* these too should be cooked alone then added just before serving.

GREEN SAUCE
(Salsa verde)

1 thick slice bread
Vinegar
1 clove garlic
2 salted anchovies or 4 fillets
50 g (1¾ oz) parsley
1 hard-boiled egg
Olive oil
Salt
Black pepper

Serve the meat cut into thick slices with boiled potatoes and the vegetables and gravy. The *salsa verde* and *mostarda* are handed round the table to be added according to taste. The remaining strained stock is usually served separately as a clear soup known as *büü* in Piedmont.

To make the green sauce, soak the bread in vinegar then squeeze out the excess liquid. Pound together the garlic, anchovies and parsley to make a thick paste then incorporate the egg and the bread. I do this in the food processor. Add enough olive oil to make a thick sauce that will be spooned rather than poured and season to taste.

BONED CHICKEN NECK STUFFED WITH BEEF
Colli di pollo ripieni

2 large slices white bread
200 mL (7 fl oz) milk
500 g (1 lb) lean beef, finely
*   minced*
1 egg
70 g (2½ oz) freshly grated
*   Parmesan cheese*
Peel and juice of 1 lemon (for speed
*   I use a zester and process the*
*   long strips of peel with the meat)*
Salt
Black pepper
3 boned chicken neck skins
Light meat stock

LEMON DRESSING

60 mL (4 tablespoons) extra virgin
*   olive oil*
30 mL (2 tablespoons) lemon juice
Salt
Black pepper

THIS IS A TRADITIONAL Tuscan recipe that is usually made with goose or chicken necks. In Florence they often serve the head by the side of the plate as decoration but thankfully I have never been faced with this delicacy!

Since only the neck skin is used as a sort of sausage casing, when necks are not available the filling can be cooked in some other casing, but the final effect is less picturesque.

Method: Remove the crusts and soak the bread in the milk. Process the meat with the egg, cheese, lemon peel and juice to form a smooth paste. Squeeze the excess milk out of the bread and mix with the paste. Season to taste.

Remove fat from the neck skin then wash and dry the skin. Tie one end very firmly with fine string and stuff, carefully avoiding any air pockets. Take care not to overstuff or the skin will split during the cooking period. Tie the second end in the same way and boil gently for 15 minutes in a light meat stock.

Serve cold as a starter cut into fine slices with the lemon dressing. (Mix together all the dressing ingredients.) The quantity can be increased and it can be served as a main course.

If this recipe is being used as a starter I like to add 1 ripe avocado, puréed with a little dressing and served in a tiny mound beside the slices of meat.

LAMB AND ARTICHOKE CASSEROLE

Fricassea di agnello con carciofi

6 artichokes
50 mL (3½ tablespoons) olive oil
4 cloves garlic, minced
800 g (1½ lb) lean lamb cut into
   cubes
100 mL (3½ fl oz) dry white wine
200 mL (7 fl oz) light stock
3 egg yolks, beaten
Juice of 2 lemons
Parsley, chopped
Salt
Black pepper

THIS TASTY LIGURIAN main course always reminds me of the Greek cuisine and I can't help wondering if some Genovese sailors brought it back from one of their many sea voyages.

Method: Remove the coarse outer leaves from the artichokes and cut into segments, removing the 'choke'. As soon as the artichokes are cut they must be rubbed with lemon and placed in a mixture of water and vinegar to prevent them going brown.

Heat the oil, add the garlic and let it begin to change colour before adding the lamb. Quickly brown the pieces of lamb on all sides then pour over the wine and after a few minutes add the boiling stock. Simmer for about 30 minutes then add the rinsed and dried artichokes.

When both the meat and artichokes are tender remove from the heat and just before serving stir in the egg yolks, lemon juice and parsley. Season to taste.

CRISPY CHOPS WITH POTATO CRUST

Bracioline di capretto in crosta di patate

2 lean kid or lamb chops per person
Salt
Black pepper
2 cloves garlic, crushed
2 teaspoons thyme
White wine, enough to cover the
    chops
3 large potatoes
30 g (1 oz) fresh breadcrumbs
Plain flour
3 eggs, beaten
Oil for deep frying

THE CRISPY COATING in this recipe from northern Italy always reminds me of the Swiss *rostli* potatoes. It is usually made with tender kid but small lamb chops work equally well.

Method: Season the chops with salt and pepper and marinate in the garlic, thyme and white wine for at least 6 hours.

When you are ready to cook the chops, peel and grate the potatoes and mix together with the breadcrumbs and a little thyme and salt.

Remove the chops from the marinade, dry well then dust with flour. Dip into the eggs then coat with the potato mixture, using a rigid spatula to press the coating into the chops. Fry in hot oil and serve at once.

PORK CHOPS WITH OLIVES

Bistecchine di maiale con le olive

30 mL (2 tablespoons) olive oil
4 cloves garlic, peeled
1 tablespoon fennel seeds
6 lean, tender pork chops, with or
    without bone
Salt
Black pepper
500 g (1 lb) peeled Italian
    tomatoes, chopped
150 g (5 oz) whole black olives,
    pitted

IN ITALY, THIS recipe from Tuscany is made with the piece of pork known as *arista*. There is an appealing story that dates the name back to the Ecumenical Council which was held in Firenze in 1438 hosted by the Medicis. The Patriarch of the Greek Orthodox Church is supposed to have praised the good Tuscan pork, exclaiming in Greek, *aristos,* meaning 'the best'. The Florentines present thought it was the Greek name for the dish and promptly rechristened the cut.

Method: Heat the oil and add the garlic. When this begins to change colour add the fennel seeds and let them 'pop' for a few minutes before putting in the seasoned chops. Brown on both sides then add the chopped tomatoes and the olives. Cook for 10 minutes then serve.

PORK FILLET WITH FENNEL AND ORANGE SAUCE

Filetto di maiale all' arancia e crema di finocchio

3 small pork fillets (tenderloins) or
   2 if large enough for 6 people
Salt
Black pepper
15 mL (1 tablespoon) ordinary
   olive oil
200 mL (7 fl oz) light stock
500 g (1 lb) fennel
Juice of 1 orange
45 mL (3 tablespoons) extra virgin
   olive oil

THE COMBINATION OF fennel and orange makes this a most interesting recipe. The finished dish is fresh and delicate with none of the heaviness often found with pork. I sometimes accentuate the flavours by serving, as a side dish, the Orange and Fennel Salad from Southern Italy (see page 50).

Method: Remove any fat from the pork and rub with a little salt and black pepper. Put in an ovenproof dish with the ordinary olive oil and the stock. Cover with aluminium foil and roast for 30 minutes, 150°C (350°F). If the fillets are bigger you may need 45 minutes. The pork must be cooked through but still very moist.

Remove any tough outer leaves from the fennel, keeping some of the feathery top as a garnish. Cut into sections and cook with a little boiling salted water until tender. Drain well and when they are really dry make a purée. Season to taste.

Whip together the orange juice and the extra virgin olive oil to make a thick cream.

When the meat is cooked cut into rounds and arrange three per person on a bed of puréed fennel. Spoon the orange sauce over the meat and decorate with some fennel feathers.

Acknowledgements

I would like to thank my family and friends who always take a keen interest in my culinary research and experiments. To the people listed below who generously shared their expertise I would like to give, *un grand abbraccio.*

Oretta Modugno, Giuseppe Menconi, Elia and Mario Longo, Maria Valentini, Sheila and Memo Damiani, Sandra della Notte, Audris d'Aragona and Alice Pugh, from the Roman Cooking School. My understanding butcher, Pino Persici, Mimo Mannocchi whose grocery store is a gastronomic treasure trove and Angelina di Mambro who still finds me the freshest herbs.

Livia and Alfonso Jaccarino, Benedetta and Fabio Picchi, Dino Casini, Alessandro Franceschetti, Fulvio Pierangelini, Gianni Carbone, Melly and Franco Solari, Giovanna and Angelo Cabani, Claudia and Tonino Verro, Emilio Baldi, Claudio Proietto, Gaetano Martini, Franco Ilari, Silverio Cineri.

INDEX

RECIPES AND NOTES

RECIPES AND NOTES

Recipes and Notes